Attention, Fool!

Kitoski, Bakaro!

Attention, Fool!

by

William J. Weissinger, Jr.
Survivor of the USS *Houston* (CA-30)

EAKIN PRESS ★ AUSTIN, TEXAS

FIRST EDITION

Published in the United States of America
By Eakin Press
A Division of Sunbelt Media, Inc.
P.O. Drawer 90159
Austin, TX 78709
email: eakinpub@sig.net

2 3 4 5 6 7 8 9

ISBN 1-57168-171-X

Library of Congress Cataloging-in-Publication Data

Weissinger, William Jacob, 1921-1988
    Attention fool! : a USS Houston crewman survives the Burma death camps / William Jacob Weissinger, Jr.
        p. cm.
    Includes bibliographical references and index.
    ISBN 1-57168-171-X
    1. Weissinger, William Jacob, 1921-1988. 2. World War, 1939-1945-
-Concentration camps—Burma. 3. World War, 1939-1945—Personal
narratives, American. 4. World War, 1939-1945—Prisoners and
prisons, Japanese. 5. Prisoners of war—United States—Biography.
6. Burma—History—Japanese occupation, 1942-1945. 7. Houston
(Cruiser : CA-30) I. Title.
D805.B9W45   1997
940.54'7252'09591—dc21   97-19294
                                                 CIP

This story is dedicated to

my wife Eunell

my children
Linda, Carla, Doug, and Peggy

my grandchildren
Scott, Steven, and Matthew Cutrer
Michael, Rebecca, and Sally Lovorn
Eric, Alex, and Amanda Weissinger

and especially to
the crew of the USS *Houston* (CA-30).

Oil painting of sinking USS Houston *(CA-30) based on a drawing by Navy Lt. Harold S. Hamlin, fellow prisoner of war. (Courtesy of Kay Hamlin)*

CONTENTS

A Note About This Book's Publication

Following the death of her husband in April 1988 and her subsequent retirement as secretary to the board of trustees of Deer Park ISD in January 1992, Eunell Weissinger was able to pursue a project that had been near and dear to her heart for a number of years.

In the early 1960s Bill Weissinger completed in longhand the first draft of a book he hoped to have printed for his family and friends. Later, a second draft with revisions was done on a manual typewriter. From there he progressed, again with revisions, to an electric typewriter. Finally, a fourth draft was done on that wonderful new invention—the computer. At that point, Bill felt that he needed to study the art of writing in order to turn out a more professional product. However, due to an initial heart attack in March 1970 and the numerous health-related problems that followed over the next eighteen years, many revisions were begun, but a new manuscript was never completed.

In 1992, with a twenty-five-year-old IBM DisplayWriter rescued from a sure trip to the trash bin by her son Doug, Eunell set up shop in a makeshift office in her home. Working with all previous drafts, revisions, and partial rewrites, Eunell went to work in earnest to glean the best from Bill's endeavors to put into readable form his experiences as a Japanese prisoner of war.

After untold hours and several computer breakdowns, and with much encouragement from her children, Eunell finally felt the manuscript was ready to be printed. She is quick to point out that every word in the final product was written by her husband. When the manuscript was completed, Eunell presented it to Eakin Press as a proposal and the book was accepted for publication.

Acknowledgments

The publishing of this book is a major miracle brought about through the efforts and generosity of many people.

First, there was Billy, who faithfully recorded his remembrance of his days as a Japanese prisoner of war.

Then, there were our surviving children, Linda, Carla, and Doug, who encouraged first their father and then me to finish the project.

There was also Kay Hamlin, wife of a fellow shipmate and prisoner of war, who granted the use of a sketch of the sinking ship done from memory by her husband, Harold S. Hamlin, and the picture of an oil painting based on that sketch.

There were fellow prisoners of war Ben Dunn, for use of his map showing the routes of Japanese ships carrying prisoners to the jungle of Burma; Frank "Foo" Fujita, for use of his artwork depicting Japanese atrocities in the various prison camps; John Wisecup, for his sketches of working and living conditions as a prisoner of the Japanese; and Otto Schwarz, for his ongoing efforts to maintain the USS *Houston* (CA-30) Survivors Association Archives and for his willingness to furnish and/or identify materials and photos.

Finally, there was Ed Eakin, owner of Eakin Press, whose decision to publish this book will be eternally appreciated by the family of William J. Weissinger, Jr.

My heartfelt thanks go to each person named for his or her role in making Bill's dream a reality.

Eunell Weissinger

PREFACE

One of my greatest desires of recent years has been that my grandchildren will remember me when I am gone with a certain amount of love and respect and with some degree of curiosity of what their old grandfather was all about. As far as the love and respect are concerned, I have no doubt as these are freely exhibited by the nine who call me Gran'pa.

One day in the early 1960s our oldest daughter Linda Kay came to me and said, "Daddy, why don't you write a book about the experiences you had in prison camp?" I began to realize this would be an excellent way to fulfill some of the curiosity I hoped my grandchildren would develop. However, I had recently read several of the stories written by my fellow prisoners of war, and it seemed to me that they had done a pretty credible job, so I wondered what there was for me to add. They had already told about the beatings, the starvation, and all the other abuses and atrocities fostered upon the hapless prisoners of the Japanese. Then it occurred to me that what they had told had been told from one person's point of view. Each story was unique because each was told by an individual who had different experiences or who wrote from a different perspective. This realization was what in the end encouraged me to tell my story.

My second, and equally as important, objective in recording my experiences as a prisoner of war is a heartfelt one: I would like for this story to be considered as an effort to commemorate the brave deeds and sacrifices of my fellow shipmates on the heavy cruiser USS *Houston* (CA-30) during the early days of the war in the Pacific, those days being the last days of 1941 and the first days of 1942.

While I had no diaries or other written notes to verify historical or factual accuracy or to refresh my memory of the events depicted and described, I did refer to books and records I had on hand for such information as names of places and dates. For the most part, however, what is written is strictly from memory; the events did happen and they are true. Thus, what is told in the following story is my personal version of three and a half incredible years as a prisoner of war of the Japanese—*as I remember them.*

BILL WEISSINGER

William Jacob Weissinger, Jr., age nineteen. Navy enlistment photo.

PROLOGUE

December 7, 1941—When I went to bed aboard the USS *Houston* (CA-30), we had just completed our fifth day in the harbor at Iloilo, Panay, a small out-of-the way seaport in the central Philippine Islands. We had arrived there on December 2 following a hasty departure from Cavite Harbor in Manila Bay where, in addition to scheduled renovations, the ship had been undergoing emergency repairs to her engines and boilers.

A great deal of renovation and modernization had been accomplished when the *Houston* spent a couple of months in Mare Island Ship Yard off the coast of California back in 1940. One of the most important tasks not completed when *Houston* was dispatched to the Asiatic Station was the addition of radar equipment. Therefore, installation of radar was definitely a high priority in the Cavite Ship Yard; and work was under way the morning of November 27 when an alarm sounded, and public address systems everywhere announced that all crewmen of the *Houston* were to report to their ship immediately.

Adm. Thomas C. Hart, commander in chief of the Asiatic Fleet, had received a message from the Office of Naval Operations in Washington that morning to the effect that diplomatic negotiations going on in Washington between the United States and Japan were deteriorating. The message went on to say that American military advisors expected that Japan would, within the next few days, initiate some sort of aggressive military action, either in the Philippines or on the Malay Peninsula, and the admiral was being advised to take appropriate action to assure the integrity of the military defense of the Philippines. One of Admiral Hart's first actions was to dispatch *Houston* to Iloilo.

The order dispatching *Houston* to Iloilo was received by Capt. Albert H. Rooks, commanding officer of the *Houston*, early on the morning of November 27, and at ten o'clock word was passed on the ship's PA system announcing that all navy yard work would be halted and the crew would begin preparing the ship for sea. Installation of radar equipment aboard the *Houston* had been foiled again.

Around half past three on the morning of December 8, I was one of eight men who left the ship to go on station as the 0400 to 0800 antisubmarine patrol. During the night Ens. John B. Nelson, the officer on our launch, told us about a radio broadcast that had come in just before we left the ship. It told of a large Japanese convoy which British reconnaissance planes had been tracking for several days. The report went on to say that unlike other convoys to Saigon which the Japanese had sent south from China and Formosa in recent months, this one had continued past Saigon and was that very morning in the Gulf of Siam.

Japanese convoys steaming south in the China Sea were nothing new; they had been doing that since July. But it was disturbing news to hear that one had gone over into the Gulf of Siam, considering the circumstances at the moment: with the *Houston* being dispatched to Iloilo and other naval units of the Asiatic Fleet having been deployed to other areas around the Philippines. The radio broadcast had indicated that the British in Malaya and in Singapore were fearful that the convoy in the Gulf of Siam indicated a possible Japanese landing on the Malay Peninsula.

Finally, it was seven-thirty and the 0800 to 1200 relief patrol should have been on its way out to relieve us. Ensign Nelson stood on the poop deck and looked through binoculars across the four miles of water that lay between us and the ship, but all he saw were undulating swells of water. It was getting close to eight o'clock, and Mr. Nelson had the signalman try to raise some response from the ship, first with his signal lamp, and then with the semaphore flags. All of us were getting anxious to get back and get our breakfast before the cooks closed the galleys.

Around eight-thirty, Ensign Nelson could see that the relief launch was finally headed in our direction. By the time it reached us, we were all really upset and ready to tell the relief crew what we thought of their being so late. As bowman, I grabbed the line from the other boat and made it secure to ours.

At once, everyone in the launch was shouting and yelling at the same time, all wanting to tell their version of what had been happening to cause their delay. The relief officer finally regained control of the situation and told us that they had been at general quarters since four o'clock and that the Japanese had bombed Pearl Harbor! Apparently, the message had come in just after we left for our patrol duty. We were stunned. Bombed Pearl Harbor? The Japanese? How could it happen? We had a thousand questions, but our relief crew had no answers. They, too, wondered how and why it had happened. It just couldn't be true. But it was.

To this day I have wondered why no one on the ship signaled to let us know what was going on; and I have always imagined that I was probably one of the last men in all the United States Navy to learn that the huge naval base at Pearl Harbor had been bombed by the Japanese.

Thus began day one of World War II aboard the cruiser *Houston*. Several books have been written detailing the ship's movements and accomplishments between then and the demise of the "Ghost of the Java Coast," a name earned by the *Houston* as a result of several announcements by the Japanese that the ship had been destroyed. My story begins, then, with the actual sinking of that gallant ship.

The news of the Battle of the Java Sea as reported in Dallas, March 15, 1942.

1

THE BATTLE OF THE JAVA SEA, AT SUNDA STRAIT

At about eleven o'clock on the night of February 28, 1942, the two remaining battleships of the hastily planned and ill-conceived ABDA Fleet (American, British, Dutch, Australian) had just entered Bantam Bay on the northwest coast of Java. Expecting to be targets of Japanese bombers when daylight came, the American heavy cruiser and the Australian light cruiser were speeding toward the north end of Sunda Strait, which runs between Java and Sumatra. The captains of USS *Houston* (CA-30) and HMAS *Perth* hoped to get their ships through the Strait and onto the Indian Ocean before the sun rose on March 1. Once there the cruisers would have more space to try to outmaneuver any falling bombs.

Suddenly, the speeding run of the ships and the hopes of the men aboard were rudely interrupted by flashing lights off *Perth*'s starboard bow. Quite unexpectedly, the cruisers had run into a Japanese landing operation: It was the beginning of Japan's invasion of Java. A Japanese destroyer patrolling the perimeter of the landing operation challenged *Perth* as she and *Houston* entered the area. The lights used in the challenging signal were unknown to *Perth*, so she answered with a salvo of six-inch shells from the forward turret of her main battery. Thus began the last battle of those two gallant ships.

Speeding and turning, firing first at one target and then an-

1

other while trying to dodge each reported torpedo, the two cruisers fought an unknown number of enemy ships. The ensuing battle lasted little more than an hour. Finally, outnumbered, outgunned, and out of ammunition, the two allied ships were sunk in Bantam Bay, off the coast of Java. HMAS *Perth* went down around midnight; USS *Houston* followed some twenty minutes later. Less than 200 men survived *Perth*; 365 survived *Houston*. The time was forty-five minutes past midnight on March 1, 1942.

When the second order to abandon ship was given aboard *Houston*, I was standing on the starboard side of the board deck forward, between the lifelines and the clip room of Number Three 1.1-inch mount. I had just dropped two water kegs into a life float which I helped provision and launch as a part of the duties of my abandon-ship station. The heavily damaged ship continued at a speed of approximately five knots, and I watched as the men manning the painter released the float to see that it didn't foul on the ship's side as it slid aft in the murky water. After the float was clear of the ship, I paused for one last look at the devastation wrought by the unanticipated attack. The entire scene was as bright as day, illuminated by three large searchlights on the Japanese destroyer positioned about 200 yards off *Houston*'s starboard beam.

Dense steam boiling from a large vent shaft from the engine room prevented a clear view beyond the after end of the boat deck. The part of the deck that I could see was almost totally unrecognizable, even though this area of the ship had been my cleaning station for the past twenty-three months. Now abandoned by their crews, the five-inch AA guns pointed at absurd angles; the ready boxes, lids open, were standing empty; spent brass from the five-inch shells littered the deck in a haphazard manner; and steam continued to pour out of the vent shaft until the entire scene was almost obscured. I saw several deep gouges in the teak deck and remembered how careful we had always been that no chip in the wood or stain had marred its appearance when the captain made his inspection tour on Saturday mornings. The metal deck portion, which was the boat storage area, looked forlorn; and I thought of the many hours, day and night, that Whitey Welbourn, 4th Division boatswains mate, had stood at the lifelines and piped the signals to the crane operators as we hoisted boats aboard in smooth weather and foul. Now there was nothing but a scattering of the debris of war appearing now and then as the cloud of steam lifted and then settled, hiding all the clutter.

This last glance had taken only seconds, and now my mind returned to the job at hand—abandon ship. I could see hundreds of men already in the water, well beyond the range of the swirling currents around the ship. Some were floating with life jackets, some were swimming without any sign of support equipment, and some were on floats or capsized boats. I had on a life jacket, so the thought of stripping off my shirt and pants was out of the question. I took off my shoes and socks, placed them neatly against the 1.1-inch handling room bulkhead, stepped over the lifelines, and jumped feet first into the water about twelve feet below. Because of the life jacket I expected a jolt when I hit the water, but I slipped in without feeling a thing—just in and down. The water was warm. Although I went deeper than I expected, it seemed to be just a second before my head broke through the surface and I could breathe again.

Looking around to get my bearings, I saw that the Japanese destroyer was still alongside, about 150 yards away, with its searchlights still beaming their bluish-white glare on *Houston*'s starboard side. To my right, aft of *Houston*, I spotted the float that I had helped launch and turned and started paddling to it. The float was already full of men, and as I swam closer they began to call out and ask if I was wounded or hurt in any way. When I responded in the negative, they began to yell that I should go out on the painter (a long rope tied to one end of the float) and help steer the float out and away from the sinking ship and clear of the searchlight beams.

There must have been at least forty men strung out the length of the painter, trying to swim and pull the float. I paddled along until I finally came to a space where I could fit in and then grabbed the painter and began to pull with the rest of the men. We had just about gotten some order along the line when heavy gunfire began to hit very close by, causing concussions from the exploding shells to slam into our stomachs. Everyone began to scatter out, trying desperately to get out of the area. Then, as suddenly as it had begun, the shelling stopped. It was then that I got my last look at "Huey Maru," the nickname that had been given to *Houston* by her crew.

The enemy destroyer was still steaming on a course that paralleled the *Houston*'s and was holding the same speed. *Houston* was receiving a literal hail of gunfire, and red rings appeared in the thin metal sides of the hanger as Japanese shells hit and penetrated. I counted six at one time. It was a curious sight. The ship was listing about twenty degrees to starboard, and there was a huge fire at the base of Number Two turret and another on the forecastle. The flag was still flying from the halyard, and there were sporadic bursts of machine-gun fire from the gun tubs atop the main mast. This last look at the Huey Maru was etched in my memory forever.

Abruptly, shells began to fall in the vicinity again, and I ducked my head into the water to get away from them if I could. I thrashed along in the warm, dark water until my lungs were gasping for air. Then I stopped, raised my head out of the water, and looked about in wonder. The searchlights had been extinguished. I could see no one and I could hear no one. The feeling washed over me that I was the only one alive; I was alone in all that water. Fear and panic engulfed me, and I again ducked my head into the water and began to work my arms and legs even more strenuously than I had before. There were no particular thoughts in my mind; I just wanted to get away from where I was.

Suddenly, I felt a light pressure on the top of my head and heard a voice saying, "Okay, sailor, take it easy. Everything is going to be okay. We're here with you. Slow down." I stopped the wild thrashing and gratefully looked up into the face of Ensign Bourgeois, division officer of the 2nd Division. The sensation of panic left me just as rapidly as it had overcome me, and I felt surprisingly calm. As I looked about, I could see that Ensign Bourgeois was accompanied by two other men that I recognized. One was a chief machinist's mate whose face was familiar but whose name I didn't know. The other was Ensign Kollmyer, junior division officer of the 4th Division. My division.

Although I had been in the navy for twenty-five months, I still felt that certain amount of awe that many enlisted men experience when in the company of their highly respected and prestigious commissioned officers. Here in the water, however, we had all been reduced more or less to the same level with one thought in mind: finding a place to land. In silent but mutual agreement, we knew we were all in the same boat, so to speak, and that we would have to work together in a spirit of cooperation.

The four of us drifted and paddled along for several minutes while the two officers discussed which would be the best direction to go. In the bright moonlight we could see the dark shape of a tall peak on Java, which we estimated was ten or fifteen miles away. We could also make out what appeared to be a small sandbar about a quarter of a mile off to our left as we looked toward the peak. The officers and the chief soon decided they were going to the sandbar. Still feeling a little uncomfortable at being the lone enlisted man in the group, I said I would head for the tall peak. The light from the moon and stars enabled us to set our directions as we exchanged "so-longs" and paddled off toward our respective destinations. No one ever saw those three men again.

I hadn't been alone in the water very long when I saw a float covered with men over to my right about twenty or thirty feet. Swimming over, I discovered again the float launched from my abandon-ship station; the one that I had abandoned earlier amid the exploding shells. Upon approaching the float, I could hear a discussion going on concerning some of the rules that were to be observed by everyone in the immediate area. The wounded and sick were to have the exclusive privilege of being inside the ring, where they could use the platform for support. If additional room existed, able-bodied men would take turns being inside for a short while. Then they would have to get out and hang on to the small line attached to the outer perimeter of the ring and let their life jackets support them.

I finally got up to the float and began to work around it, trying to find a place where I could get a hold on the line. Among the men I recognized there were Isaac Black, seaman first class, 4th Division; Edward Carlyle, seaman first class, 4th Division; Joe Alleva, rate and division unknown; Lt. Joe Dalton, division officer, 5th Division; and Joseph Whaley, seaman first class, 4th Division. Joseph "Bennie Boy" Whaley hailed from Harlan County, Kentucky. "Ben," as most everyone called him, had been in charge of the cleaning gear locker, and he and I had been pretty good friends. I can't recall that we ever made any liberties together, but we did talk and work together aboard the

ship. Both of us were very glad to have found a 4th Division
shipmate.

The float was rated to accommodate twenty men, but there
were quite a few more than that number in and around it. The
canvas-covered balsa wood ring that provided flotation was a
foot or eighteen inches under the surface of the water. The flotation ring was oval in shape and measured about eight feet overall along the long dimension and about five feet overall along
the short dimension. A slatted wooden platform about two feet
wide and five feet long was suspended from the float by white
cotton cords and served as a floor to the hole in the middle of
the float. A quarter-inch manila rope that was attached to the
outside of the oval ring at several places was used by men as a
hand line to hang on to. Ben Whaley and I were among those
hanging on. We greeted each other, then began to pay attention
to the discussion that continued in the float. It seemed everyone
had a different idea about how the crew of the float should be
organized. The one officer aboard, Lt. Joe Dalton, was from Ok-
lahoma. It didn't take too long for him to get things organized.

About an hour had passed since I had gotten in the water.
In the hazy moonlight it was easy to see people all around, but
everyone spoke quietly, as though a loud sound might disturb
the neighbors. A fire blazed brightly for about thirty minutes off
to the right, and it was speculated that a tanker had been hit and
was burning.

As the float drifted along, all its users began to try to think of
ways to make faster progress. The idea of towing it by swimming
with the painter had been given up when it was found that this
method took too much energy. For a while the men hanging on
the hand line tried kicking their feet while pushing on the after
end of the float, thinking that might move it faster; but that effort
was abandoned, too, when no progress was discernible. The float
had been equipped with two aluminum oars, but one of them had
gotten lost in the confusion of dodging falling shells and trying to
get away from the sinking ship. Someone tried rowing with the
one remaining oar, but that didn't work either. Then someone
else came up with the idea of using the oar for a mast and a skivvy
shirt for a sail. This idea seemed to have some merit, but problems arose immediately. There was nothing to use for mast stays

or to tie the "sail" to the mast. Besides that, there was only an occasional light breeze, not enough wind to use a sail. We would just have to depend on the tides and currents to propel the float. Destination: the tall peak, some ten or more miles away. We drifted in silence.

Soon Ben and I decided that we might do better if we began to look for our own method of getting to the peak. We talked it over for just a minute, then agreed that we'd swim out from the float and see what we could find. We hadn't gone too far, perhaps fifty or sixty feet, when we discovered two floating objects. One was a brass can about two feet square and eight inches thick. The other was an empty five-inch shell canister about three and a half feet long and about six inches in diameter. Ben chose the canister and left me with the brass can.

The fun really began when Ben tried to mount the canister. He started by pushing one end underwater, slipping it between his legs, and then pulling himself along until he was near the center of the canister's length. He did fairly well as long as a portion of his life jacket was in the water; it acted somewhat as a stabilizer. But the second he got the jacket clear of the water, he lost his stability and over he would go. He made several attempts as I offered encouragement from the comfortable position I had on the gas can. I had shoved the can underwater and then thrown myself across it, belly-down. The can stayed below the water, but it gave me enough lift so that I was partly out of the water and could breathe fairly easily. Ben's antics soon caught the attention of those on the float, and they began to cheer him on. The entire escapade had the appearance of a rodeo of sorts and was to serve as our only relief from the stressful situation we were in.

We had been in the water for nearly two hours and were beginning to suffer the consequences of the lack of sleep, infrequent eating, and overexertion of the past few weeks. Slowly but surely, fatigue overcame us as we continued our pursuit of the distant seashore.

Suddenly, a deathly quiet fell over the area of the float, and all heads turned toward the barely detectable low gurgle of a boat motor. We all held our breath as we peered through the misty haze that was hanging just above the water. Then there it was, the white hull of a launch not more than ten feet away. A muffled bumping noise and movements that seemed eerie gave evidence that there were several people in the launch. Then the throttle was cut and the engine speed was reduced. Soft voices spoke in an unintelligible language, faint figures moved back and forth, and finally there was a splash. The launch idled slowly past us. When it was some twenty feet away, the motor picked up speed and the specterlike hull with its gurgling exhaust melted into the haze. When the sound of this mysterious passerby was no more, everyone breathed a sigh of relief. All aboard the float came to the same conclusion: It was the Japanese looking for their own. From all appearances, they never gave our float a moment's notice.

About the time the tension was easing from one near encounter with enemy personnel, someone shouted, "Look over there!" To our left and approaching at a speed of about ten knots was a Japanese troop transport. From our observation point low in the water, the ship looked as huge as a mountain—and it was headed directly for us. Ben and I left our cans and began trying to swim out of the big ship's path. When it got to within about fifty yards, we could see that it was rigged with paravanes and that it was going to be impossible for us to get beyond their reach. We were caught. All we could do was try to dodge the bow of the ship and hope and pray that the cables connected to the paravanes were set deep enough not to catch our legs.

By this time the ship was upon us. We relaxed as the upper cables went over our heads and the ship passed about twenty feet from us. As it slid by, we could see troops standing on the hatch covers amidship and could hear them singing what we supposed was a Japanese army song. We were close enough to feel the turbulence of the ship's screw, but we felt no current drawing us down. As the transport disappeared into the darkness, Ben and I breathed a little easier and began to wonder what had happened to the float and the men who were on it.

We paddled along together for perhaps half an hour, bumping into various individuals and groups every now and then. No one spoke, and it was quite an eerie feeling. I supposed that everyone had been shocked as much as we had by the passing of the ship and were taking time to silently thank God that they had been spared. We had given up all hope of ever seeing the float and its crew again when suddenly we saw a tall figure standing on the water and heard a loud voice saying, "*Stroke!*

Stroke! Stroke!" As we drew nearer, we discovered that the man who seemed to be standing on the water was Lieutenant Dalton. After nearly being run down by the Japanese transport, the guys on our float decided they really needed to get the hell out of the water, and onto land. Everyone was swimming alongside the float, taking their strokes as Lieutenant Dalton called cadence. Ben and I managed to grab hold and got in on a few minutes of the heave-ho effort, an effort that lasted no more than ten minutes or so. The three nights without sleep, combined with three hours of fighting to stay afloat, were beginning to sap what little energy had resulted from the rush of adrenaline we experienced during the brief battle.

Everyone began to get quiet again, and several of those inside the float drifted off to sleep. Those of us hanging to the hand line couldn't afford that luxury, so we spent our time contemplating our arrival on foreign soil. We had no idea at that time what kind of force we had encountered in the sea battle. The possibility of a landing force being present was probably the last thought on anyone's mind. So we speculated that the fires we could see on the beach were being tended by the native Javanese. At the time, we thought we could reach land in another couple of hours and were looking forward to a friendly welcome.

Gradually, dawn began to break, and we were amazed to see some six or eight troop transports off to our right with a busy scurrying of small boats around each one. Floating nearer to us was all kinds of debris, and among all that flotsam we could make out a human head here and there. A human form was quite close to us, perhaps within thirty yards. It appeared that the drifting man was asleep, supported by his life jacket. After our shouts failed to produce any response, Isaac Black volunteered to swim over to investigate. He shook the man, lifted his head, and then just let it drop. When Isaac returned to the float, he said it was Martinez, one of our shipmates of the 4th Division, and that he was dead. We never knew if he died of wounds or exposure. We just left him drifting slowly away on the water.

The discovery of Martinez had a sobering effect on all of us. Up until then, I'd had no thought of death. Now I realized that we had not been playing a simple game of tag the night before.

2

FIRST PERSONAL ENCOUNTER
WITH THE JAPANESE

By now the sun had risen above the water, and it seemed we were no closer to land than we were at dawn's first light some two hours before. Getting to land became a real point of concern. But what to do? The idea of rigging a sail would work no better now than it had earlier. The water looked like a huge mirror with light swells here and there, and there was still no wind. Our one ray of hope seemed to be the barge-type boats we could see running between the ships and the shore. Surely one of them would eventually come out to us. Eventually, one did. It was a rather strange-looking craft resembling what the Filipinos called a banka boat. It was double-ended and had a motor in it. The boat was manned by two people, a coxswain and an engineer.

As the boat approached, Lieutenant Dalton told everybody to get rid of anything that might identify our ship. Most of us had left the ship fully clothed, so we began to feel in all our pockets. I came up with a thoroughly soaked half pack of cigarettes and a book of matches bearing a picture of the ship and the name *Houston* spelled out in silver ink. Several of the others found they, too, had the matchbooks. We eased them into the water undetected, we hoped, by the two Japanese men in the boat that was approaching some fifty feet away.

The engineer took the boat out of gear and glided up to our float. The coxswain positioned the boat so that the float was along its starboard side. The engineer took hold of the painter and made it fast to a cleat on the boat, then both men gestured that we were to board their craft. As we climbed over the gunwales, we were motioned to sit on the deck amidship. The thwarts ran parallel to the gunwales and not athwart-ship as they do in American launches. We were facing aft, looking at the coxswain. Suddenly, he barked out, "Ingerish! You Ingerish!"

Lieutenant Dalton answered, "No, American, we American."

"No American, Ingerish! *Bakaro!* (fool)" the coxswain shouted. Then he waved his arm around to indicate all the area of Java and the Java Sea and said, "Ingerish all, no America, all Ingerish!"

"Well, buddy, have it your way," said Lieutenant Dalton as he looked back over his crew from the float.

In the meantime, some of us began to remove our life jackets, which by that time felt as though they weighed a couple hundred pounds. However, the engineer slapped one guy's hand and motioned to let us know that we were to keep the jackets on. Then, surprisingly, both the engineer and the coxswain began to offer us cigarettes and a light.

When we were picked up, we were about a mile and a half or two miles from the transport ships; so the ride over to the first one lasted some fifteen or twenty minutes. After the short conversation and the handing out of cigarettes, the rest of the trip was made in silence. I felt sure that everyone was wondering what fate had in store for us when we reached the larger ships. It wasn't very long before we found out, and what fate had for us at that moment was definitely a surprise.

The coxswain first approached the transport nearest the beach. He skidded the board into the foot of the gangway as the engineer cut the engine, then jumped out of the boat and jogged up to the main deck. He saluted a man standing at the head of the gangway and began to talk to him. Then he disappeared from our view as he went inboard. About five minutes later the coxswain came skipping down the gangway, leapt across the gunwales and onto his platform at the stern of the boat, and took hold of the tiller. As he was positioning himself, the engineer started the motor, a bell rang, and we were under way again.

We pulled up to a second ship. The routine was the same:

skip up the gangway, talk to a man we supposed was the officer of the day, go inboard, reappear a few minutes later, down the gangway, start the motor, and away we'd go. This routine was repeated four times with one exception. At the fourth stop, rather than getting under way again, we were ordered to stand up. We took this to mean that we were going to board this transport; but when the first foot hit the gangway platform, I think it belonged to Lieutenant Dalton, a loud scream resounded from the coxswain. He began to motion that we were to leave the boat by jumping off the stern into the water. The idea was that we were to become floating castaways. Our float had been released and was drifting away very quickly. In single file we stepped across the small platform at the stern of the boat and stepped off into the water. The first couple of guys who went into the water caught the float and held it until the rest of us got there.

As we made our way to the float, we could see that three Japanese soldiers standing on the ship's main deck were eyeing us very closely. A single thought seemed to strike us all at about the same time: We were released so some of the soldiers could have a little rifle practice. We had been told many times that the Japanese didn't take prisoners of war. So we all tried to swim to a position where the float would be between us and the ship. The soldiers never took their eyes off us and walked slowly aft on the deck as we drifted and swam in the current. This period of anxiety and wondering lasted for five or six minutes before we felt that we were out of range of the rifles. The enemy never made a move to shoot at us. They just ambled along, dragging their rifles, butt down, along the deck.

Just as we began to feel some relief from this tense situation, we heard aircraft engines. Looking up in the direction we were drifting, we discovered three Zeros coming in about 200 feet above the water. The planes banked to their right and headed in our direction. We thought: What a hell of a way to go—as targets for flying aircraft! As the Zeros made their approach, we all crowded to the side of the float and did our best to stay under the water. We must have presented a comical sight because it's not easy to go underwater, much less stay there, with a life jacket on. The planes approached very quickly, zoomed overhead with the pilots leaning over the cockpits, went past us a mile or so, banked to the left, and began to gain altitude. Apparently, the pilots were just looking over the situation. Not a shot was fired.

As we tried to reorganize, we heard a loud explosion and felt a ripple of concussion run past us in the water. About five miles ahead, a geyser of water erupted from the stern of a Japanese destroyer, which immediately got under way. From what we could make out, the explosion occurred as the destroyer was dead in the water.

We began to speculate as to what was going on. My greatest hope was that they had sent a diver down, had found the *Houston*, and had somehow hit the primer of the five-inch shell that had been left in the jammed rammer of Gun 3. Whatever the cause, the explosion and the destroyer speeding away remained an unsolved mystery.

3

STRUGGLE AGAINST THE ELEMENTS

It had been an exciting hour and was now about noon. We had been in the water for some twelve hours, and exhaustion was really taking its toll. Our principal need was to get ashore as quickly as possible. The prospects now looked very good, for we could see breakers foaming their way to the sandy beach about a mile or two to the south. If we looked closely, we could just make out people walking along the beach. All we had to do now was paddle through the surf and make our landing.

"Everybody swim!" Lieutenant Dalton called out. Immediately everyone outside the float swam to the seaward side and began to try to push the float toward the beach. Sometime later we knew that we were still only moving with the tide or the current. We were running parallel to the beach at about five to seven knots and had not gotten one inch closer to the shore.

This struggle of men against a very strong tide and current went on for about two hours. All the while, we were drifting to the west toward Sunda Strait. Finally, at an estimated time of two in the afternoon, we were in the mouth of the Strait. From that location we could see both Java and Sumatra with what appeared to be a long, wide river separating them.

Extending from each shoreline toward the middle of the Strait were outcroppings of rocks with a scattering of sandbars here and there. Some of the bars were almost large enough to be called islands themselves. As our float was swept by the current, it was driven toward the Sumatra side of the Strait. At one point it seemed that the float would be swept right onto the rocks, so we all hung on and let it run with the tide. When we got to within a couple of hundred yards from the rocks, the current changed and we were swept out toward the center of the Strait again. The change in direction caught us unaware, and by the time we noticed what was happening, our efforts to get the float out of the currents and in near the beach were in vain. The tide and current seemed to have us in their grip and would not release us.

The Strait, where it meets the Java Sea, was probably five miles wide. When we were near the beach of Sumatra, the Java beach could hardly be seen. We were surprised at the speed with which we crossed the Strait and how rapidly we seemed to be approaching the Java beach. But when we got within 800 to 1,000 yards of the Java beach, the current began to carry us directly down the Strait. It seemed there was no way for us to get any closer to shore, no matter what we did. By this time it was about three in the afternoon. We had been swimming, trying to push, pull, do anything that we could to get the float out of the current, with no luck at all.

We were taking a break and trying to decide what to try next when we spotted some debris floating nearby. One of the fellows swam over to the pile and discovered a crate of onions among the scraps of timber, cane, and ropes. He managed to get the crate free of the morass and floated it over to us. It didn't take too long to break a couple of the slats on the crate and get to the onions. I got two about the size of my fist. They were the best thing I had eaten in a long time.

It was quite agonizing to be able to see the breakers rolling in on the white sandy beach of Java and not be able to get to it, but that was what was happening. Try as we did, we could not get over the invisible barrier that separated the current running in the Strait from the water rolling in to break in huge waves on the beach. We ate our onions, drifted down the Strait, and rested. We were becoming very weak and knew that we'd have to get on land soon or we would not have the strength to do anything.

Talk got around to having someone swim in to the beach

and see if he could find someone to come out in a boat and pick
us up. It was felt that perhaps one man without his water-laden
life jacket could get over this barrier, whatever it was, and get on
the beach. At first, Lieutenant Dalton was against the plan. He
said we had all been together too long now for anyone to risk
losing his life. He felt that in time the tide or the current would
favor us and get us to the beach. But two men, Isaac Black and
Edward Carlyle, put up such a strong argument that Lieutenant
Dalton finally agreed to let them try. They felt certain they
could make it to shore with no trouble.

The daring men shed their life jackets and stood up on the
ring of the float. Carlyle dived in first; Black followed just seconds later. We watched as they took steady strokes, staying close
together for only a few minutes. Then Carlyle began to drift to
the south faster than Black. In a couple of minutes they were
about a hundred yards away from the float. Carlyle was approximately fifty yards south of Black. In the meantime, some of the
guys had again gotten behind the float and started trying to
push it toward the beach. It seemed that the current was now
causing us to drift in that direction, and the men wanted to take
advantage of every bit of space we could gain.

All of a sudden, it was obvious that we were indeed in a current that was carrying us toward the beach, for as we watched the
swimmers we could see that we were drawing even with them.
Black was about 500 yards south and to our right; Carlyle, now
just a small speck, must have been at least a mile south of us. We
were about 600 yards from the beach and going at a pretty fast
clip. We passed Black. We could see that he was in trouble and
could hear him yelling, but we couldn't make out what he was
saying. What should we do? At that very instant a fishing boat
was seen coming in our direction. It was decided that we would
hold our position, if we could, and that as soon as the fishing
boat got to us, we'd go out and pick up Black.

It took about five minutes for the fisherman to reach us.
When he came alongside the float, there was a mad scramble as
all twenty-six of us tried to get into the boat at the same time. It
was a fairly small boat and we doubted that it would hold all of
us for one trip—but it did. The old Javanese man who was sail-

ing the boat was flooded with five-, ten-, and twenty-dollar bills from the grateful crew of the float.

As soon as the commotion died down two or three minutes later, we made him understand that we had another man in the water behind us. He headed his boat in the direction we indicated, but when we reached the point where we thought Black should be, we could see nothing or no one. To our south we could see Carlyle in a banka boat, sitting in the stem, rowing for all he was worth. At least we knew—or thought we did—that he was safe. We continued searching for Black for about ten minutes, and when we couldn't find him, sadly told the fisherman to go on to the beach. We never saw Black or Carlyle again.

4

ASHORE AT LAST ON JAVA BEACH

As soon as the fishing boat reached shallow water, everyone began to climb out and wade to the beach. We didn't realize how weak our legs were until we tried to take the first few steps. Several men fell down in the water and had to be helped onto the dry land. We staggered some twenty or thirty feet into a coconut grove, where some lay down on the sand while others leaned on the trees.

A small group of Javanese boys were there to greet us and immediately wanted to know if we would like them to cut down some of the coconuts for us. We had some previous experience with coconuts in the Philippines and knew that the green coconut milk was a good thirst quencher. We also knew that too much of the milk from a green coconut was an excellent laxative. At the moment we really didn't care what happened. We just wanted food and drink. Within a couple of minutes there were coconuts lying all over the place. A Javanese boy would pick up a coconut and with a quick slash of his bolo knife cut through the husk and just enough of the shell to make a small hole for the milk to run out. I must have drunk the milk of three or four coconuts before I stopped to breathe. I knew what the results were likely to be, but I didn't care.

Lieutenant Dalton got his share of the Javanese refreshments, but his main concern was contacting local or Dutch authorities. While we gathered around the boys opening the co-

conuts, he was trying to get information about where the nearest village was, who its leader was, and where his residence or office was located. He questioned several of the Javanese on the
beach and finally found one who could understand English, as
well as the importance of our precarious situation. Presently,
Lieutenant Dalton called out for our attention and announced
that we were to follow him and the Javanese who would lead us
to the home of the village magistrate.

We left the beach and walked a couple of hundred feet up
a sandy trail to a paved road. We turned left and almost immediately were in a populated area. There were houses along both
sides of the street, much like any small American community.
We walked along the street for about three blocks before coming to a house that was set approximately a hundred feet back
from the road. Standing on the lawn was the magistrate and his
family, which consisted of a wife and two or three children. The
man was of Chinese descent. He stood about five and a half feet
tall and was dressed in a white shirt and dark trousers. Fortunately, he spoke English.

The first question Lieutenant Dalton asked the magistrate
was, "What is the name of this village?" I don't remember the
name the man gave, but he also said that the town of Labuhan
was twenty-eight kilometers south and that there were some
units of the Dutch army there. Next, the lieutenant asked if
there was any food the family could give us. The magistrate
translated for his wife then replied that they didn't have very
much but that his wife would prepare what they had.

While the food was being cooked, we lay about on the grass
and speculated on what our fate would be now. The magistrate
had told Lieutenant Dalton that the Japanese had made a landing on the Java Sea side of the island, about fifty kilometers as
the crow flies from where we were, and that the people of his village were expecting their arrival at any moment.

In a very short time the magistrate's wife and a couple of the
children came out with the food they had prepared: three very
small chickens and half a dozen bottles of some kind of soft drink.
This meager fare was divided between twenty-six very hungry
sailors. I got a few bites off a drumstick and a swallow of the soft
drink. It didn't satisfy my appetite, but it was appreciated. The
food was consumed in just seconds, and then a conference was

held to decide what our next move should be. We knew the Japanese were on Java. We knew, or thought we knew, that they could be in this village momentarily. We knew that Labuhan was twenty-eight kilometers south and that the road going to it was paved, and we had been told that the Dutch army had some personnel there.

The sun had sunk lower and lower as we ate and talked. It was going to be completely dark in just minutes. We had to get organized while we could still see what we were doing. As the facts were sorted and discussed, we reached a decision to start walking toward Labuhan immediately. This idea was a sorry prospect for a group of men who had just reached land after spending some nineteen hours in the water, struggling the whole time to stay afloat. And our feet: What were we to do about covering for our bare feet? They were as tender as an open wound after having been soaked in salt water for more than nineteen hours. Some of us had carried our life jackets up from the beach, so we began to rip them apart to fashion some sort of protection. Ben and I ripped off the collars of our jackets then cut strings from the longer sections of the vests and tied them around our feet, using some of the kapok filling as padding. Several of the others did the same thing, but some of the guys thought they could walk without any protection and were ready to go.

The plan was that we would walk one hour and rest ten minutes. Somehow, someone had a watch that still worked. Also, we would stay in a single group so we would at least have strength in numbers if anything came up that would require group action. We intended to travel in military style, with Lieutenant Dalton walking at the head of the column along with a couple of the petty officers who were with us.

While we had been busy figuring out what we were going to do, a large crowd gathered on the magistrate's lawn. By the time we were ready to leave, we had plenty of guides to see that we got on the right road. The residents were anxious for us to leave, and it was evident that they didn't want us to come back. Although there was only the one paved road through their little village, each one of them appointed himself as a guide and led us out of town.

5

We had walked less than half a mile when our jury-rigged shoes fell apart. But Ben and I were among the luckier ones. We were "deck-apes" and aboard ship we had run around barefooted most of the time. We also had waded in salt water much of the time, so our feet were reasonably tough, despite their recent prolonged soaking. Walking on the pavement proved no real difficulty. It was only when we stepped on a small pebble with sharp edges that we had any real pain. We kicked off what was left of our "shoes" and strode to the head of the column.

Within minutes after we got on the paved road, it became pitch dark. Tree limbs met above the road and blocked out most of the moonlight, and we could hardly see anything to the sides of the road. Every once in a while we could make out a small house or outbuilding that had been built by the road, but most of the time it was like walking in a dark tunnel with splotches of moonlight acting as small spotlights to show where the paving was.

By the time we finished the first hour, my legs felt like two sticks of wood. They were so stiff I could hardly bend my knees. Lieutenant Dalton turned to face the men behind him, calling out softly, "Break time. Let's take a ten minute break." Ben and I hit the ground like a ton of lead. Like everybody else, we were practically dead on our feet.

I must have dozed for just a minute, and the next thing I

21

remember hearing was Lieutenant Dalton and one of the petty officers saying that we were going to make different arrangements. It seemed that some of the guys were just getting to the rest area when the ten minutes was up. This was throwing everything off schedule. Lieutenant Dalton made a decision. He said it was quite apparent that there were some of us who could walk faster than others, so he thought it would be okay if the fast walkers went on ahead at their own speed. If they ran into any kind of trouble, they were to all come back to the main body or at least try to send somebody back to inform the ones who would be walking slower. It was agreed that this would be the order of things, and Ben and I struck out with two or three of the others who had been in the "fast group."

We of the faster group didn't take another rest break until dawn. We walked at different paces, but we never stopped. As the first glimmer of dawn began to light the sky, we could see on the side of the road ahead what appeared to be several campfires. We stopped to listen but could hear nothing. We walked closer. When we were some two to three hundred feet from the clearing, we could see that it was a small *kampong* (a grouping of native huts) and that there were bodies everywhere. Some were lying on the ground, some on small stoops in front of the half dozen or so huts, and some in the shallow ditch alongside the road.

We were in a quandary. Who were these people? Were they Japanese? Slowly and cautiously we approached one of the bodies in the ditch, and when we got about five feet from it the body rose up and said, "Hi-ya, mate." It was one of the sailors off *Perth*! Of course, we didn't know that right away. In fact, we hadn't even given much thought at all to the *Perth* and her crew. Our thoughts had been purely personal—thoughts of our own welfare. We were just as surprised to find Australian sailors lying along the road in Java as they were to be found by Yank sailors. An instant later the Aussie jumped to his feet and shouted loud enough for the whole world to hear, "Hey, mates, the Yanks are here!" That did it. Within seconds the whole *kampong* was alive with moving bodies. It seemed they were coming from everywhere, and the sight they presented was appalling.

There were at least forty Aussies in the group, and most of them had the misfortune of floating through pools of fuel oil while trying to reach shore. There were a few clean ones among them, but most were covered with oil—and were naked. It was a sight that was pitiful and at the same time comical. Their hair was matted down with big globs of oil. Their eyes in the firelight glowed like red coals; and as they moved, they resembled black scarecrows come to life. But their appearance did not dampen their enthusiasm when they found they had Yanks in their presence.

In talking with the Aussies, we discovered that because *Perth* had abandoned ship before *Houston*, they had gone down Sunda Strait ahead of us. Their experience had been much the same as ours, except that they had been forced to drift farther down the Strait than we had. They arrived at this *kampong* about the same time we landed twenty-eight kilometers to the north. The Javanese who lived here had given them what food they had, sweet cakes and tea—plenty of tea—which was brewing at the moment in the five-gallon kerosene tins the sweet cakes had been stored in. They had been allowed to spend the night in the *kampong*. By the time we got there, all the Javanese had left, and the Aussie sailors had the whole place to themselves.

Dawn was just breaking when we arrived at the *kampong*, and we talked and drank the hot tea and ate the sweet cakes until the sun was well above the trees. At this time Lieutenant Dalton and the guys who had stayed with him through the night came into the makeshift camp. He told us that he didn't know how many of our crew were behind him. He said they had made a couple of stops during the night and that each time they got ready to move on, some stayed back—preferring to sleep rather than to try taking another step toward finding the Dutch forces. The lieutenant added that as much as he regretted it, he had to admit that from now on every man was on his own. Apparently, there were no Australian navy officers in the camp. As we talked, we all looked to Lieutenant Dalton for direction, some of us half wishing he would turn us loose to be on our own. When he did, Ben and I began to make our own plans.

It was quite obvious by now that there were no Dutch forces in this area. Nevertheless, by some means, word began to circulate that the Dutch army had a post set up in a small town about fifteen kilometers inland to the east. Ben and I decided to start out in that direction. We looked around and asked if anyone wanted to go with us. A couple of the guys said they were ready to go. We said "so-long" to Lieutenant Dalton and told him that if we found any Dutch authorities, we would tell them he was ashore and where we had last seen him. He said that he would do the same for us. Then with a handshake, we headed off down the road. It was now around nine-thirty or ten o'clock on the morning of March 2, 1942.

6

COOL RECEPTION FROM THE JAVANESE

Our small group walked along wondering what had happened to the rest of the *Houston* crew. We wondered if we would ever see them again or if there was a chance that we had been the only ones to get to the beach. We had walked about two miles when we spotted a rather large bamboo and *atap* hut on the left side of the road. It was the first building we had seen since we left the *kampong* except for a few we'd seen during the night—the ones that sat shaded from the moonlight and had no distinguishing features. Our curiosity was aroused, so we opened a door and went into the hut.

Once inside it was easy to see that this was some sort of a local bar or beer joint. Extending from the wall that was next to the road was a long bar. The remainder of the room had tables and chairs and an area that probably served as a dance floor. It looked very much like the small bars and beer joints in any small town in America. But what was a place like this doing here on the west end of Java?

Unfortunately, the man behind the counter couldn't or wouldn't speak English, so we were not able to question him about it. Eventually, by gesturing and pointing, the man offered us a drink of water from a large wooden keg sitting on one end of the counter. We had been repeatedly warned about drinking unboiled water or eating any uncooked food, so we hesitated a

moment before deciding to drink up anyway. At least our thirst
was quenched for the time being.

We spent some ten or fifteen minutes in the bar, and just as
we came out we spotted a pony cart coming down the road from
the same direction we had come. In the Philippines, such a con-
traption is known as a *carameta*. An old man was driving the cart
and we hailed him. He spoke to us in Javanese and pointed in
the direction he was going. Of course we didn't understand a
word the old fellow said, but one of our guys gave us his own in-
terpretation. He said, "The old man said, 'Do you want to meet
a nice girl?'" This was a standing joke because a sailor is always
supposed to be looking for a nice girl. It made no difference
that the old man had no idea that we were sailors. He probably
knew we were not Dutch and figured we were some kind of
tourists. Then, too, he may well have known a lot more than we
gave him credit for right then.

Anyway, we all nodded our heads to show that we agreed
with whatever he said and boarded the cart through a little door
at the rear. The cart had a canopy on it, and it felt good to be
riding in the shade with a cool breeze created as the little pony
trotted along.

Suddenly, one of the guys had a brilliant idea. In the Philippines when we rode *carametas*, and were usually pretty well under the influence, one of the things we would do was get two or
three of us on the rear step of the cart and lean way back. This
action would lift the shafts on each side of the pony, which in
turn lifted the harness, which would, in many cases, lift the pony
off the ground. If it didn't lift the pony off the ground, it would
certainly make him light on his feet; and it was a jolly sight to
see the excited pony trying to get his feet back on the ground
and the excited driver trying to get his rambunctious fares out
of the *carameta*. We got the same reaction on the road in Java.
The old man became quite upset. He grabbed the whip out of
its socket and before we realized what was happening had gotten in a couple of pretty telling blows on Ben, who had the misfortune to be sitting on a seat just behind the driver. It took a
few minutes, but we did manage to get the old man calmed
down. After convincing him that we wouldn't do that again, we
continued on our ride. We realized that riding was a lot easier

than all the walking we had been doing since setting foot on Java, and we were sorry we had caused the old man trouble.

We had traveled approximately five or six miles after leaving the bar when we rounded a curve and discovered that every other one of the huge trees that lined each side of the road had been felled directly across the road to create a tank barrier. Upon reaching the first tree, the old man stopped the cart, shook his head, and said something in Javanese. About a mile ahead we could see red tile roofs that we thought might be houses. We gestured to the old man that we would carry the cart across the tree trunks if he would walk the pony. He climbed down from his seat, unhitched the pony, and led it over the trunk of the tree. With two men on each side, we grabbed hold of the wheel spokes, got everything balanced, and sidled along, lifting the wheels clear of the first tree trunk when we got to it. It was about eighty to a hundred feet to the next tree, so a couple of us held on to the shafts and drug the light cart down to it. The procedure was repeated. The old man led his pony over the trunk, we lifted the cart over, and the old man smiled.

We found that the cart wasn't as light the second time as it had seemed the first time. As we straightened up to go to the next tree, someone said, "Hell, fellows, we can walk to that town a lot easier without toting that cart along. Let's go." So off we went. I looked back after we had leaped over a couple of the trees. The old man was standing there and yelling. He was speaking Javanese, but the meaning was coming through loud and clear. His shouting was soon swallowed up in the foliage as we continued to leap over trees and proceeded toward the buildings.

Just at the edge of the town was a small creek that had a bridge to carry the road. However, the floor had been blasted out of the bridge, and debris from the explosion had landed on the roof of a house about 200 feet from the town side of the creek. The red tiles had been completely shattered and the house, like all the other buildings in the immediate vicinity of the bridge, was totally vacant. At first we thought the bridge had been bombed, but as we got closer we could see that charges had been set to create the damage. We were afraid to try to walk on the framework of the bridge floor, so had to go down to the wa-

ter in order to cross the creek. There was enough debris in the
water to form a walkway across the narrow creek, and we were
able to cross to the other side without getting our feet wet.

When we climbed the creek bank and looked down on the
street, not a person was in sight. There were very few houses
along the street, and what little we could see was like a ghost
town. We walked along speaking softly to one another as if we
expected at any moment to be set upon by someone we couldn't
see but who, we felt sure, was watching us. It was quite an eerie
feeling.

About a thousand feet from the creek we came to a street that
intersected and dead-ended at the street we were on. To our left
we could see some kind of activity on the next street over, about
500 feet away. We turned on the side street and upon reaching
the corner could see a big crowd milling around the front of a
rather ornate building. We headed that way, and as we got close
to the crowd we began to recognize a few faces. We had run into
another group of survivors from *Houston* and *Perth*!

We asked one of the fellows standing there what was going
on. He told us that the building was the local constabulary, and
that some of the officers of *Houston* and *Perth* had gone inside to
speak to the magistrate about getting food, clothing, and medical supplies for the guys who needed them.

The four of us who had been together since early morning
became separated as we found shipmates we had been more
closely acquainted with aboard ship. However, Ben and I stuck
pretty close together. We asked some of those who were there
how they had gotten to this place, but they were unable to give
us any details. They said they had been directed along different
roads and had just ended up in this little town.

As we stood and talked and became reacquainted with guys
from the ship, there was considerable activity around the front
of the constabulary. Uniformed men that we took to be officers
of the local or provincial police force came and went constantly.
After about thirty minutes, the front door opened and the magistrate came out onto the portico. He was Chinese, stood about
five feet tall, and was rather chubby. He was dressed in a west-
ern-style business suit, and there was absolutely nothing of oriental influence about his clothing. The magistrate was followed

by the officers who had gone into the building to talk with him. One of *Houston*'s officers, John Nelson, told the *Houston* sailors who gathered around him as he came out to the street that the magistrate was going with all the survivors to the public *godowns* (warehouses) to get the clothing, food, and medical supplies that had been asked of him.

With the magistrate at the head of the procession, some one hundred or so survivors walked down the street in a fairly orderly fashion. The Javanese who were present made way for us, but we began to notice a look of concern on their faces as we turned a corner and began to walk toward the *godowns*.

The *godowns* consisted of four rather long, narrow buildings approximately two hundred feet long by thirty or so feet wide. The sides were corrugated tin and the roofs were *atap*. Across from the *godowns* was a large open area resembling a playing field, possibly a soccer field. As we got to within thirty or forty feet of the *godowns*, the Javanese who had been making way for us began to crowd in, filtering between us; and coming across the open field was a horde of people headed in our direction. Now the magistrate was before the first *godown*, and as he reached to open the door a murmur went through the crowd of Javanese. Although the sound they made was soft, the expression was one that created a measure of fear in all of us.

One Javanese man standing shoulder to shoulder with Red Conner was eyeing a gold crucifix on a thin gold chain that Red wore around his neck. Over in the middle of the crowd, another Javanese jostled his way to the magistrate. Presently, he was face to face with the magistrate and began to speak loudly and gesture with widely swinging arms. After a few minutes of conversation with the excited man, the magistrate stretched up on the tips of his toes and said as loudly as he could, "The people do not want you to have the things you asked for. They say it is their property and that you should see the Dutch army to get what you need. I am sorry but I can't open the *godown*. I cannot give you clothing or medicine. I am sorry."

Just as the magistrate had begun to speak, the Javanese who had been eyeing the little gold cross lashed out with his right hand and jerked the chain from Red's neck. Now, Red had been on the fight team aboard ship and as a natural reaction doubled up his fist and drew back to deliver a fast blow to the man's face. Immediately another hand came through the crush of bodies and restrained him. The hand belonged to one of the local provincial policemen. He said, "Let him have it. Don't fight him." Then we noticed that several Javanese men who were standing nearby had their *krises* (daggers) unsheathed and were ready to begin slashing the moment Red's fist hit the Javanese man's face. We realized that the policeman had saved our lives and most probably had prevented a massacre right there. The latter realization came to us sometime later, after we had been captured by the Japanese and were recalling the incident.

The hopes of getting clothing and food having been dashed by the Javanese crowd, the magistrate said everyone should go back to the constabulary building and he would see if he could do something else. As the crowd—now turned mob—broke up, it dawned on us that we had been outnumbered by the Javanese by about three or four to one. If any trouble had started, we would not have stood a chance. We ambled back to the constabulary, the effects of exhaustion and disappointment beginning to get to us. Also, we were becoming very anxious to find some Dutch authority. So far we had seen none.

We arrived back at the constabulary just in time to be summoned up to the steps of the portico, where we were given a five-gallon can resembling a common kerosene can and told to leave the area as soon as possible. We had no idea what was in the can, but we took it and walked down the street that ran directly away from the front of the building. After we had gone only a block or so, we came to a set of railroad tracks. Someone suggested that perhaps the tracks would lead us to Batavia, the capital of Java. We stopped a young Javanese boy and asked which way it was to Batavia. While he didn't seem to understand the question, he did understand the word "Batavia." He pointed up the tracks to his left and said, "Batavia." We turned in that direction and began to walk down the tracks and out of the town.

7

LOOKING FOR BATAVIA AND THE DUTCH ARMY

Very shortly after we started walking along the tracks, we realized that they served as a boulevard for pedestrian traffic and were actually crowded with foot traffic going in both directions. However, any Javanese that saw us coming would quickly cross to the opposite side of the tracks until we passed by.

We were now a group of six, but I can remember only a couple of the names. One, of course, was Ben Whaley, my shipmate from Kentucky. The other was a musician by the name of John Porter. Porter's main concern after we were on the railroad track was to find something to drink. It was awfully hot and we'd had nothing to eat or drink for several hours. Every few steps, Porter would say, "We're going to dehydrate and fall down in a dead faint if we don't get something to drink soon." We listened to him complain until we had walked some three or four miles out of the town and were crossing a small culvert with a narrow stream running under it.

Someone suddenly got the bright idea that we could empty the can we'd been carrying and boil some water in it. Everyone agreed this was a good idea, so we went down a small embankment to the edge of the stream. Then we walked a little way into the brush and found a nice shady spot with plenty of room to build a fire. We pulled off the lid of the can and found that it was full of tiny tea cakes about half an inch in diameter with a sugar-

31

like frosting. We emptied the tea cakes on the rocks, and someone waded into the stream and filled the can about half full of water. Someone else found suitable rocks and piled them up for the can to rest on. And from somewhere, another person produced a fire under the can. We knew we would have to drink from the can, but we were well on our way to taking care of the dehydration problem. It wasn't too long before we realized that we might as well take advantage of the time it would take for the water to boil and get ourselves a bath.

All six of us had come off the ship with some kind of clothing. Ben and I had on the marine shirts and trousers that had been issued to the gun crews to serve as flash protection. Porter, who had been on duty as a hospital corpsman's aide at a battle dressing station, was wearing dungarees. We had not washed the salt water out of our clothes since arriving on the beach; and now that we had time to notice, they did seem a bit stiff. So, clothes and all, we went into the stream where the cool water was very refreshing.

It seemed to be just a short while before our drinking water began to boil. We let it boil for about ten minutes then wadded up a shirt, picked the can up off the fire, and set it in the middle of the little stream to cool. While we waited, we continued to take advantage of the coolness of the stream. Soon the water had cooled enough that everyone could drink his fill of the warm liquid. Each of us had eaten a few of the tea cakes and crammed our pockets full, but we felt that the sugary coating would just make us thirstier and left the bigger part of the pile on the bank of the stream. Now we were ready to begin the trek to Batavia in earnest.

We got back on the railroad tracks and began to walk along in single file, as seemed to be the custom with the Javanese. The sun was really bearing down when all of a sudden a rain shower began. All the rain appeared to be coming out of a very small cloud; but instantly it was coming down in sheets, as the saying goes, and we began to look for shelter. Our desire to get out of the rain was just a natural reaction, I suppose. We talked about it later, and no one could come up with a good reason why we had suddenly run for the shelter of a shed which stood beside a small house about a hundred feet from the tracks. The shed was about the size of a double-car garage, and we ran through a door which was only partly open. It was dark inside and for a few minutes we couldn't see anything. We were making jokes about our reaction to the rain when we began to regain our eyesight and could see two Javanese boys huddled in one corner. They appeared to be about eighteen or nineteen years old, and the expression on their faces told us that we weren't really welcome to share their shelter.

Gathering in a small group near the door, we talked the situation over for a minute or two. We decided that maybe, if we showed that we had no bad intentions, we could break the ice. So one of our group looked in their direction, smiled, and said, "Pretty hard rain, isn't it?" Their reaction: deeper scowls. Automatically, instantaneously, and unanimously, we recognized that we were not welcome under any circumstances. We left just as we had arrived—speedily. It was after we got back to the trail along the railroad tracks that we began to question whose idea it was that we needed shelter from a simple little rain shower, for now the rain was over and the sun was shining again.

We must have walked some eight or ten miles from the town where the magistrate tried to help us when we came to a paved road that crossed the railroad. As we approached the intersection, we began to wonder if there would be any advantage in taking the paved road. Certainly, it would be easier walking. Just as we got to the road and were still trying to make up our minds, we heard someone shouting. The road ran up a slight hill and, like the road we had been on earlier that morning, had trees felled across it. A Javanese boy was running and leaping over the trees as he came down the hill. He was calling, "Are you American sailors? Are you American sailors?"

Someone in our group said, "How the hell would he know that? It must be a trick." When the boy was only a few feet from us, we asked him how he knew that we might be American sailors. He said that in the nearby town there were many American sailors and that he had been sent to tell us they were waiting for us. Still a little doubtful, we stood trying to make up our minds whether or not we should believe him. Suddenly, the boy said, "Cigarette? You like cigarette?" We all answered at once,

"Yeah." Then we decided maybe he was telling us the truth and told him we would follow him to the town.

We still felt a little anxious as we trudged up the hill but thought that we might as well go with him since we were tired and hungry, and the Dutch seemed to have left the island anyway.

As we topped the hill, we could see that we were in a fair-sized town. We had walked a few blocks when we came to the town square, which very much resembled the county seat in any small community in America. Various kinds of stores lined all four sides of the square, and in the center was a building that reminded me of the courthouse in Seguin, Texas. Why I should have thought of Seguin at that time, I did not know. I'd only been to that Texas town a couple of times in my whole life. Nevertheless, that thought went through my mind as I looked at the building. We passed a ladies clothing store, and on a corner near it was an auto repair shop. All the shops were closed. The streets were empty, not a soul in sight, much like a small country town on a Sunday afternoon.

About a block past this square we came upon another square with the appearance of a park. Green grass covered all the flat area, and a number of trees seemed appropriately situated for picnic areas. A concrete sidewalk went completely around the park, which was about 300 feet square. Directly in the center of the square was a building that looked somewhat like a residence. On closer inspection, however, it appeared to be some sort of clubhouse or community center. On each side of the building a walkway ran from the outer encircling sidewalk to a set of steps leading to a wide double door. A veranda approximately ten feet wide, three feet high, and fronted by thick, well-pruned shrubs went completely around the structure.

As we got about halfway between the sidewalk and the building, we began to recognize faces in the crowd of people on the veranda, and they began to recognize us. There was a great deal of shouting back and forth as we went up the steps. We were still greeting shipmates when a white-coated attendant came and told us that he would bring us some rice and tea if we would stay where we were. We said, "Bring on the chow." Suddenly, we felt in a sort of jovial mood. I suppose it was because we had found out that there were others who were in the same shape as ourselves, or maybe it was just that we felt we had been rescued from something. Whatever caused it, the mood continued for several hours while more shipmates continued to straggle in until well after dark.

I ate the food that was brought to me: a bowl of clean, hot, white rice with half a boiled egg on it and a cup of hot tea. Then I went into the large main room in the center of the building to see who else I could find that had made it off the ship and who, like myself, had the good fortune to make it this far. The reuniting of shipmates and the swapping of stories of the various experiences of the day went on until nearly midnight. By now our ship had been sunk for almost twenty-four hours. It was still March 2, 1942, but soon to be March 3.

The structure that was being used as a haven by the survivors of *Houston* and *Perth* appeared to have been some kind of a meeting hall. Four smaller rooms approximately twenty feet square were situated off each corner of the larger center room. Somehow or another, I got into one of the anterooms and was able to claim the only piece of furniture that I ever saw in the whole building. A small vanity bench about sixteen inches wide and two and a half feet long was my bed for that night. Total fatigue had finally gotten the best of me, and I managed to curl up on that small space where I slept until just after dawn.

Although I was vaguely aware of people jostling around in the room and loud talking each time another *Houston* or *Perth* survivor was brought in, I awakened in the morning feeling fairly well refreshed, if somewhat cramped. As I gradually became aware of where I was, I could tell there was some kind of excitement in the air. The main room was completely filled to the point of being jam-packed, and a worried-sounding murmur rippled through the room.

I got off my "bed" and could only get as far as the door to the main room, where I could see some of the officers looking out the wider doors that opened onto the veranda. I asked what was going on, and someone standing nearby said that the natives had surrounded the building. The officers were looking out at the crowd of Javanese that did, in fact, completely encircle the building we were in. They were standing three to four deep on the sidewalk that formed the perimeter of the park. They were saying nothing that could be heard by us, just standing and staring at the building. The officers were trying to determine if their mood was friendly or hostile. After some of the experiences we had the day before, we were becoming leery of the native people. The seemingly cordial Javanese who had so graciously attended to our need of food the night before were now gone. We had no one to act as interpreter, for no one in our crowd could speak Javanese or Malay.

After thirty minutes or so of consultation, the officers of *Houston* and *Perth* decided that we would form up in a column and march out four abreast. A couple of the *Houston* officers still carried their sidearms. The .45-caliber pistols were actually useless after being submerged in salt water for several hours. But maybe the people out there didn't know that, and maybe the sight of the pistols would act as a deterrent to any violence. At least it was the consensus of our officers that it was worth a try, because we had to leave the building somehow. It took a little time and some doing to get the eight or ten officers positioned near the door so they could go out four abreast. Finally, on the count of three, the doors were opened and the officers began their march across the veranda, down the steps, and out toward the mass of Javanese on the sidewalk.

Four by four the men formed up as the column snaked outside. I got into the column about ten or twelve ranks behind the officers and was, I knew, quite wide-eyed as the leading rank of officers got closer and closer to the Javanese who hadn't moved an inch as the column approached. However, as the first rank got to within one stride, the Javanese saw that the column had no intention of stopping and parted to let us pass through the solid ring they had formed to the street.

It had been decided during the earlier consultation period that if the Javanese resisted our leaving the building and the property on which it stood, we would try to assemble back inside the building. If, however, they offered no resistance and we could get to the street, the column would turn right and march in a military manner up the street and out of town, with our destination being Batavia. So when the column did reach the street, the order "COLUMN RIGHT! MARCH!" was delivered in his best military manner by Ens. John B. Nelson, USN. The leading ranks turned to the right as the last ranks were coming out of

the building. As soon as the full column was in the street, the order "COLUMN HALT!" was given. The officers then ran back
along the column warning everyone to stay together and to not
break ranks.

We had marched no more than half a mile when again we
heard the order "COLUMN HALT!" The column was beginning to fall apart because of the inability of some of the men to
keep up with the marching pace that had been set by the leaders. We stood there for just an instant, waiting for the others to
catch up, when someone near me said in a loud, hoarse whisper,
"Let's go." Five or six men broke ranks and headed for a trail
between the shanties that were off to our right. Like a flash, Ben
and I were right behind them. We ran some fifty or sixty feet
and I could hear the sound of someone running behind us.
Thinking we were being chased, but not wanting to take time to
look back, Ben and I tried to run a little faster to catch up with
the men who had first broken away from the column.

Suddenly, we couldn't help breaking out in a laugh as we
ran. We were pretty close to some of the little houses and were
able to catch the surprised looks on the faces, mostly of children,
at the doors and windows of the shanties. Chickens were
squawking and flapping their wings, trying to get out of our way.
And there were a lot of barking dogs running after us and the
chickens. I was reminded very much of some of the *Our Gang*
comedies I had seen as a young boy back in San Antonio, Texas.
I didn't know what made Ben laugh; maybe the scene reminded
him of something in his childhood days in Kentucky.

We must have run for at least ten minutes. Once clear of the
little houses, we ran through the stock pens behind them,
through gardens and a small orchard, and out onto one of the
narrow paths that ran between the rice paddies. Our route began to rise and we were soon at the foot of a mountain. It was
the tall peak we had kept our eyes on two nights before as we
drifted in Bantam Bay. Then we were past the rice paddies and
approaching a very narrow trail, one that seemed only wide
enough to accommodate two-wheeled carts. It was much too
narrow for automobiles or trucks. Soon we were going up a
rather steep rise, where we caught up with the leaders. Now we
discovered that the footsteps we had heard behind us earlier be-

longed to two more of the guys who had also had all they wanted of the marching column. Ten of us gathered under a small
tree beside the cart trail. There were six American sailors and
four Australians.

Lounging in the shade for a few minutes, we tried to get our
breath back while getting acquainted. As we introduced ourselves to the Australian sailors and they to us, a wrinkled, feeble-
looking old Javanese man came out to the bamboo fence at the
side of the trail and made some sort of gesture that we took to
mean he was offering us food. We nodded our heads and said
"Yes," for we'd had no breakfast and were truly hungry. The
man emitted a sound somewhere between a gurgle and a
squeak, and almost immediately two young fellows appearing to
be around ten or eleven years old came out of the little shack
that stood some thirty feet behind the fence. The old man spoke
to them and then patted them on the head. They ran to a coconut tree behind the shack and climbed up as if they were walking on a broad sidewalk. It always amazed me to see how fast the
people of southeast Asia could go up a coconut tree. In a matter
of minutes the boys had seven or eight of the green coconuts on
the ground. Then they came down just as quickly as they had
gone up and very shortly gave the coconuts to us, husks clipped
and the little holes there so we could drink the milk.

We sat there for perhaps twenty or thirty minutes, expecting
any moment to see someone coming through the rice paddies
and up the trail to get us and take us back to the larger group. But
there was no movement in the paddies except that of the Javanese, who seemed to be going somewhere all the time.

We discussed what our objective should be, but we couldn't
come up with anything because we didn't know where we were
and we didn't know the way to Batavia. At the time, we didn't really take the Japanese into consideration. Finally, we decided to
just follow the trail to the top of the mountain. Maybe when we
got there we could get a better view of the situation and make
further plans. So we began our trudge up the steep road.

We would walk a mile or so and then stop under a tree to
rest. Each time we stopped, someone would come—seemingly
from nowhere—and offer us food and drink. We had coconuts,
bananas, papayas, mangoes, and peanuts along with coconut

milk, water, and some sort of Javanese drink which we could not identify. We figured it was a soft drink or some kind of brew. Whatever it was, it did a fine job of quenching our thirst. As for the water, by this time we didn't much care whether it was boiled or not.

As the sun rose higher, we began to wish we had hats. We all had clothes of sorts. Ben and I had our marine khakis. Red Conner, the fellow who lost the crucifix, had his dungarees. The other three Americans had on shorts they had acquired since coming ashore, and the Australians were all wearing sarongs they had been given the night before to cover their nakedness. But no one had a hat. At one of the stops we made, we asked by gesture for some kind of cloth to wipe the sweat from our foreheads. Each of us was given a small hand towel which we tried to fashion into a hat. There wasn't enough material in them to do the job, so we just draped them over our heads. This trick worked to a certain degree. At least we got a little relief from the sun's rays that by then were really bearing down.

No one had a watch, but we reached the peak of the mountain around noon by our estimation and could see all of Bantam Bay. We could see the Japanese transport ships anchored in a neat row about two miles offshore. The total distance from where we stood was probably close to ten miles or more, and we couldn't make out any boats going between the ships and the shore. I tried, as I was sure the others did too, to picture what the scene looked like from our present vantage point on the night the battle took place. Also, I tried to imagine where the *Houston* lay on the bottom of the bay but couldn't begin to determine where the spot might be, since I hardly knew where the ship was when I was on board. Furthermore, from atop this mountain it was plain to see that Bantam Bay involved a lot of water.

After reliving the experience of two nights before from this lofty vantage point, we continued down the road. Now the pitch of our trail was downward, and it seemed to be even harder to walk going down than it was when we were climbing up.

We had made only a couple of rest stops when we came to two wooden cottages on the right side of the road. A picket fence ran across the front with one wide gate that served both houses. Sitting on the front porch of the house on the left were three men and a boy of about twelve. Two of the men appeared to be in their late twenties or early thirties and the other looked to be in his late sixties. We left the road, which was wider on this side of the mountain than it had been on the other side, and headed for the gate. About the time we got to the fence line, the older man stood up and began to bow from the waist. Rather reluctantly and with motions that showed they were unsure of what to do, the other two men got up and began to copy the movements of the old man. The boy just strolled out away from the house and came to meet us. The three men began to speak in a language we couldn't understand and continued to bow. Their conduct struck us as being rather funny, and we began to grin and say to them in English, "Hey, don't bow to us. All we want is something to drink."

Surprisingly, the old man understood English, for he replied, "We thought you were from the Japanese."

"No, we're American and Australian sailors looking for the Dutch army," one of our number replied.

The two younger men now resumed their seats on the porch and made no effort to join the conversation.

"You say you're thirsty?" the old man asked.

"Yes, we've been walking for a good while now and we were hoping that you might have something to drink here," one of my shipmates replied.

The conversation continued for several minutes while we and the old man sort of felt one another out. We learned that the three men were leaders of some sort of religious organization and that the houses were, in effect, parsonages. The two younger men lived in the house where they were sitting. The older man lived in the house to the right.

After the man was satisfied that we were indeed what we represented ourselves to be, he offered to give us something to drink. As we headed toward his house, he suggested that we have something to eat as well. He said, "I've got some native cheese I think you'll like. It's made with goat's milk." We entered the house through the back door and went through the kitchen and into a room that seemed to serve double duty. It was a dining room and a den or library, for there were bookcases on two walls. When we saw the books, we asked if he might have a map of Java so we could find out where we were now and where Batavia was. He said he did have such a map and went to one of the bookcases and pulled out an atlas, which he handed to one of us. He said, "I'll get the cheese while you look the map over. And help yourselves to the oranges. They're fresh mandarin oranges. They came off the trees just out the window there." He had hardly gotten the words out of his mouth when a loud cry came from the back yard—a cry filled with alarm and urgency.

We looked out the window and saw the young boy running as fast as he could toward the house, calling out his message in Javanese or Malay. The old man dropped the cutting board he was going to use to slice the cheese and ran to the window to converse with the boy. Speaking rapidly, the boy turned and pointed down the road in the direction we had been traveling. The old man translated and told us that the boy had just said that Japanese troops were coming in our direction. They were only a kilometer away and should be coming to the houses any minute. Then he turned and began to speak to the boy again. When he had finished the short conversation, he turned to us and said, "You must leave. Go out the back door and take the trail up the steep hill there. The boy will show you the way."

The sudden realization that Japanese troops were only minutes away set our adrenaline to flowing. We stormed out the back door and found the boy waiting near the back fence and motioning for us to follow him. We leaped over the fence, and immediately the ground began to rise. It was almost a vertical climb, but there was a path so we supposed it was the regular way to go up the hill. At the moment, however, it looked like a sheer cliff one thousand feet high.

Someone yelled out, "THE JAPS ARE COMING, TAKE TO THE HILLS!" and like a flock of parrots we all began to yell the same words until we found we needed all our breath to climb the hill. Silence came quickly. The path was narrow now and we had to go single file. No one wanted to bring up the rear. Later I imagined that we looked like a rolling ball of arms and legs as each man struggled, first, to stay on the trail and, second, to avoid being the last one in line.

In only a minute or so we came to a sort of plateau. It was a fairly level piece of ground, and the bamboo huts of a *kampong* occupied the biggest part of the area. There were probably about a dozen huts there and they were all empty. As we looked around to get ourselves oriented, we heard the boy yell, "I have to go now." Then we saw his head disappear over the edge of the plateau.

"Well, what the hell are we supposed to do now?" asked Alex Wolos. We had a quick conference and reasoned that the Japanese, in all probability, wouldn't come up the hill right away. Surely, we thought, it would be safe to stay where we were. After coming to this conclusion, we decided that as long as we were going to be here, we ought to investigate the huts and see if we could find anything of value. The investigation took all of five minutes, as it was plain to see that whoever had lived there had taken everything but the dirt floors and the huts themselves. It also appeared that the huts had only recently been vacated, perhaps that very morning.

Straight ahead and about half a mile away as we had come over the plateau, the ground began to drop out of sight and the ever-present rice paddies appeared. The empty huts were to the right of the trail running up the hill. To the left was a combined garden and banana grove that was surrounded by a bamboo picket fence. We walked over to the area and sat down, leaning against the fence. The sun had gone behind some clouds and it was shady now. We knew we had to make some plans soon. We gave some more thought to our situation and came to the same conclusion we had reached earlier—for the moment, we should stay where we were.

About the time we decided that we might go see if there were any green bananas in the grove about fifty feet behind us, we heard a male voice ask, "Can I be of any help?" We turned and looked into the face of a Javanese boy who appeared to be about eighteen years old. He spoke very clear English. That surprised us, so we asked him how it was that he could speak the language so well. He told us that he had been going to school in Holland and that he had learned it there.

After this short conversation, he said he would help us find ripe bananas, but by that time we decided maybe we ought to get on the road to Batavia. After all, that was what we wanted and needed to do. The boy said he would lead us through the rice paddies to a road that would take us to Batavia. We told him to lead off.

The boy took us around the garden and banana grove and onto a narrow trail through some clumps of bamboo. There we saw yet another *kampong*. It, like the one we had just left, was uninhabited. Hanging from a tree was a rope swing, so we all took turns swinging once or twice before we got on one of the narrow paths that went through the rice paddies. This little trail offered scenery the likes of which I had never seen before, nor would ever see again. From our position on the plateau we could look down the mountainside, and as far as the eye could see were the terraced rice paddies. The ponds, or paddies, were about fifty feet square with narrow dikes separating them. Running along the side of the trail we were on was part of the water system. It consisted of a bamboo tube about six inches in diameter. Through the tube, water was pumped from a stream at the bottom of the mountain to the uppermost paddy. When this paddy was flooded, the excess water ran through a slit in the dike and fell into the next lower paddy, and so on right down the mountainside. The rice in the paddies was about a foot tall and was the brightest and freshest-looking green I had ever seen. At least at the time it certainly was impressive. I had neither the time nor the inclination to count the paddies, but there must have been several hundred in view. The combination of shade, the symmetry of the paddies, and the bright color of the rice made a picture that I would never forget.

We wound back and forth through the paddies for nearly an hour, walking along on the path which was on top of the dikes, the trail leading us steadily downhill. Finally the boy led us along the top of a dike that led to a weedy area to one side of the paddies. He stepped off the dike and disappeared in the weeds that were more than head high. When we hesitated, he called out from somewhere in the weeds, "Come this way." We went into the weeds where he had bent them down as he entered, and soon we had him in sight again. We walked on another twenty or thirty yards through the tall weeds, then abruptly walked right out of the weeds and found ourselves on a paved road. The road came as a surprise because we had never caught sight of it as we wended our way down the mountainside, so we had no idea we were anywhere near a road.

When we had all stepped out onto the pavement, our guide

ducked back into the weeds as though he wanted to hide from someone. Then he said, "This is as far as I can go with you. Stay on the paved road. It goes to Batavia. Just stay on the pavement." Even as we looked, he disappeared through the weeds and we were left to our own devices again.

8

CAPTIVES OF THE JAPANESE

In the direction that the boy had indicated we saw that the road made a curve to the left about a quarter of a mile ahead. On the left side of the road, just at the curve, we saw what seemed to be a combination gasoline station and grocery store. To the right were wooden houses. Again, the familiar scene was very much like any small-town setting in America. I couldn't get over how similar our present surroundings were to their American counterparts.

We walked up to the little store and went in. Inside we found that it was arranged in much the same fashion that a grocery store back home might be. There were a few bins of fresh vegetables and shelves of canned goods and a familiar-looking cash register on the counter. We wandered through the small store but didn't buy anything until we found the candy counter and some bottled liquid that we thought was some kind of soft drink. We made our selections then went to pay for the goods with our American dollars. We gave no particular thought to the fact that our money might not be accepted here. However, when we presented the American bills to the girl behind the counter, she acted as though she'd never seen them before. Probably she hadn't. Everyone scraped around until we finally came up with enough Dutch guilders to pay for what we had.

When we went outside again, Wolos opened the bottle of

liquid he thought was a soft drink, took a little taste, and made a face. He said it was too sweet for him and that he thought it was some kind of concentrate.

While we had been inside the store, a group of some fifteen or twenty of the local citizens of the little town had gathered across the road. There were five or six small children in the crowd; and when we came out, they just stood in place and stared at us. We didn't give their scrutiny a lot of thought. We had just about become used to being looked upon as curiosities, so we weren't paying much attention when one of the little kids came over to Wolos and gestured that he wanted the bottle Wolos held. We thought it was kind of comical, as did the local citizens. We all got a laugh out of the kid's actions. Wolos handed him the bottle and the kid looked like he had just won the world. It was quite evident that the little boy knew what to do with the liquid in the bottle.

As this little bit of action was going on, we had wandered out to the center of the road. Now we turned and walked in the direction we hoped would take us to Batavia. When we got some distance from the store, we noticed that the Javanese who had been watching us had also gotten in the road and were starting to follow us. We had gone no more than a quarter of a mile, with the group of natives maintaining a distance of about 200 feet, when we came to a rise in the road. We couldn't see up the road until we got over the six- or seven-foot rise; then, at first, we couldn't distinguish anything unusual in our surroundings.

For some distance the land around us was flat and level and, like all flat land we had seen in Java, was covered with rice paddies. Groves of trees rimmed the paddies, and beyond the trees there seemed to be some low hills. Then we noticed some bamboo buildings that appeared to have been only recently constructed about a mile straight down the road and off to the right side. The buildings were surrounded by a fence, and just off the road in front of them was a tall flagpole with a banner at the top. We'd never seen such a flag or banner before and it was quite a puzzle to us. We talked for a while, trying to decide what the large white field with a big red ball in the center could mean.

A few suggestions were offered as to what the flag was or what it signified, but none of them satisfied everyone. We decided that one of us had to go to the buildings and find out what it meant. Alex Wolos had made the most intriguing suggestion. He spoke with a certain tone of authority when he said, "I know what that flag is. It designates that the Dutch army high command is having a meeting." He was questioned on that opinion, and it was called to his attention that there was no Dutch flag flying. If the Dutch army was there, why didn't they display their national colors? A few minutes of discussion ensued, but Wolos remained adamant concerning his opinion.

Someone finally said, "Okay, sailor, if you know so much, why don't you go up there and tell the Dutch command we are out here?"

"Okay, I will," Wolos rejoined.

With the discussion ended, he turned and started to walk toward the buildings with the enigmatic flag.

As Wolos walked off, we sat down beside the road at the lower end of the rise. Every few minutes one of us would stand up and look over the top. Five minutes passed, then ten. Still no sign of Wolos. In the meantime, the Javanese who had followed us from the little store remained standing in a tight little group about twenty feet behind us. We tried to speak with them, but they would just look at each other and giggle when we directed any question at them.

Finally, someone stood up and looked up the road. He squinted a bit and then said, "He's coming back." We all jumped to our feet and looked up the road. Sure enough, Wolos was sauntering in our direction. His pace was slow and easy, as though he didn't have any place to go and no certain time to get there. That was a sign to us that he had been right—the Dutch were there. But when Wolos was close enough to speak to us, he said, "It's the Japs. They said to tell you that if you value your life you will form up into a squad and march in and surrender."

Upon hearing this news, we began to review our situation to see if we had any other options. It seemed clear now that the Javanese behind us would prevent our going back the way we had come. To the left and right of the road were the acres and acres of flat, level areas with nothing taller than the one-foot-high rice paddies. There seemed no way to escape unseen across the paddies to the trees a mile or so on the other side. We discussed the possibility of just staying where we were until after dark, some three hours away, and then trying to get to the trees and the hills behind them. The one fly in the ointment was—the Japanese knew where we were. Finally, not able to comprehend all the implications of the meaning of surrender, but having a strong desire to continue living, we decided that we had no alternative. We had to surrender.

We formed into a squad, two ranks, four abreast, with two of the Australian sailors in a third rank, and began to march toward our soon-to-be captors. As we walked, someone suggested that maybe it would be a good idea if we got rid of anything that could be perceived as a weapon. There were a couple of splashes as pocketknives were tossed over into the water of the rice paddy to the left. Conner took the .45-caliber automatic out of his pocket, released the clip into his hand, shelled the bullets out one at a time, and tossed them into the paddy. Then he kissed the gun and gave it a strong heave. It landed about twenty feet away with a sickening splash. Only a few drops of water flew into the air marking the spot where it landed. Then he said, "Well, hell, I might as well get rid of this, too." He jerked off his "Mae West" and just dropped it on the side of the road.

We were now about a quarter of a mile from the buildings and could see quite a bit of activity around them. Spread across the road directly ahead were four Japanese soldiers with rifles at port arms. A fifth soldier was standing in front of them. They were all watching as we continued to march toward them. When we got within ten to fifteen feet of them, a voice called out, "DE-TAIL, HALT, ONE, TWO!" We were shocked, for the command had come from the Japanese soldier standing in front of the open rank of four soldiers. Nevertheless, just as if it happened every day, we came to a very respectable halt. Next we heard the command "DETAIL, OPEN RANKS, ONE, TWO!" Again, as if it were a regular occurrence, we opened ranks. The Aussies had a little trouble with this command because their military routine was somewhat different. The rest of us, however, had no problem. The American military routine for open ranks is for the front rank to take one step forward and then for each man to space himself one arm's length away from the man next to him. The purpose of this maneuver is to allow an inspecting officer to pass completely around each individual in the formation. The Japanese soldier, a sergeant, did exactly that.

He walked in front of the first rank, reaching into pockets, patting their legs, and speaking very good English. He asked if there was anyone from California who lived in the vicinity of Stanford University. He said that he had attended classes there until a little more than a year ago. He told us that he had gone home to Japan on a vacation and had been drafted into the army and had been unable to return to the United States. It happened that one of the *Houston* sailors had lived in that part of California and was familiar with the towns around the university. The sergeant asked a few questions about certain "gin mills," as he called them, and seemed amused to find out that the sailor had patronized some of them during the same time the sergeant himself had been in California. He said to the sailor, "Perhaps we have seen each other before, na?" He continued his search as he talked, and now it was my turn. He reached into my pockets. Empty. Then he ran a finger down into my watch pocket and brought out a twenty-dollar bill. I was just as surprised to see it as he was. "Well, well, a twenty-dollar bill. I haven't seen one of these in several days." He handed it back to me as he said, "Here, you'll probably need this," and passed on to the next man.

As soon as I saw the bill, my mind returned to a scene that had taken place aboard ship about a week before. It was early evening, the sun was right on the horizon, and the watch of the guns was being changed. I was going on watch and Harold Justice, a shipmate of the 4th Division, was coming off watch. Justice came up to me and said, "How about a stake? How much can you lend me? I want to get in that roulette game in the aerologists' shack." I pulled a ten and a five out of my billfold and handed them to him. Justice was an incurable gambler. Anytime there was any betting going on, he was part of it. It made no difference if it was odds on a baseball game, a game of cards, rolling dice, or roulette—he was there. There was only one problem: he usually didn't have the money to get into the action. Over the months we had been together aboard ship, I had begun to supply him with his stakes. He always repaid the minute his winnings would allow it. The rate was six for five. That is, for every five dollars I loaned him, he would repay six. That particular evening he had taken the fifteen dollars and dashed up the ladder to the flight deck to get in the game. He came to Gun 1, my watch station, about thirty minutes later and gave me a twenty-dollar bill. He said, "Here, this is the smallest I have. We can work out the difference later." He was anxious to repay the stake and we had made this kind of arrangement before. I had completely forgotten about the bill until the Japanese sergeant pulled it out of my watch pocket.

The sergeant completed his inspection and returned to his place in front of us. He said, "Now I want you to go over to that truck, get up in the bed, and stand there. DETAIL, FALL OUT!" We broke ranks and started to stroll over to the truck. The four soldiers with the rifles separated so that we could pass through them and then began to operate the bolts of their rifles. They had to load them. One little private who stood about four and a half feet tall was off to the side of all the activity, and he was having a terrible time. He couldn't get the clip of ammunition to go into the magazine. Wolos broke away from our group, went over to the frustrated private, took the gun out of his hands, grabbed the clip and shoved it down into the magazine, rammed the bolt home, and handed the rifle back to the stunned little soldier. Then he broke into a trot and leaped up on the bed of the truck. This action created a flurry of excitement because the instant Wolos broke into a trot, the soldiers thought he was trying to escape. There were a couple of loud shouts as rifles were raised. Then they saw what was really happening. It took only an instant, but it was a rather tense instant.

Ben and I were the first to reach the truck. Already in the bed were six or seven Javanese men varying in age from teens to old men. One old man was lying in the center of the bed, and it didn't take an expert to tell that he was deathly ill. Ben and I climbed over the tailgate and went all the way forward to a position just behind the cab. The others got aboard and stood along the sideboards. There were two trucks. We were in the lead one. We waited for several minutes as Javanese men continued to come out of the buildings and climb aboard the trucks. Finally, we heard a lot of shouting and there was some bustling about as two soldiers—one carrying a huge Japanese flag and rifle and the other only a rifle—came to our truck, jumped into the bed, trod right over the sick old man, and came forward. The one with the rifle grabbed my shoulder and shoved me to one side, then treated Ben to the same bit of persuasion.

When it was apparent that they were going to run right over the old man, hob-nailed boots and all, someone tried to push the soldiers over. For his trouble, he got a shove with a rifle butt. So in the span of just a few seconds, we were introduced to Japanese brutality—conduct that we were to learn was considered normal by their troops, but something that not even three and a half years of experience could make us feel was civilized, much less normal.

It took about ten minutes for the Japanese to get the trucks loaded. There were more civilian prisoners than military; but then we were just a windfall, so to speak. They hadn't been expecting to have to haul us. The guard who had climbed up onto the truck with a rifle leaned over the sideboard and yelled something to the sergeant who had searched us. The sergeant yelled back. The driver, a Javanese civilian, started the motor, put the truck into low gear, and we got off to a bucking start. The truck behind us followed suit, staying some fifty or sixty feet behind us.

I noticed that we were going up a hill and that just beyond the shrubs and scrubby brush on the right shoulder of the road there was a high bluff that formed one side of a valley that seemed to be about three or four miles wide. The floor of the valley some 700 feet below us was one huge rice field. The other side of the valley was formed by high hills that had the invariable rice paddies terraced up their sides. But the bluff at the edge of the road was what really caught my attention.

During the months we had been on Asiatic Station, we had briefing sessions at various times. It had been emphasized in these sessions that the Japanese army took no prisoners of war. That thought came to mind as I looked at the bluff at the side of the road, and I told Whaley that I thought we had better get a good look at the scenery because it was beginning to look like it would be the last we would see on this earth. He agreed. Most of our companions probably had the same thoughts, though I never heard any of them say so. To my mind, the setup was perfect. They would line us up along the bluff, shoot us, and let our bodies fall to the bottom of the bluff. At the time I had no real fear. I just began wondering if it would hurt when they shot us.

We had gone only about two or three miles when we noticed that the driver of the second truck was slowing down and honking the horn. At first, our guards didn't notice. When they did, they began to beat on the roof of the cab and scream like madmen. The driver of our truck obediently pulled over to the side of the road. The two guards were quite agitated that the other truck was so far behind us and kept leaning over and yelling at the driver and the other officer in the cab. It was only about five minutes before the driver of the rear truck honked his horn and began to come closer to us. I thought, *This is it. As soon as the other truck gets here, they'll unload us, back us up to the bluff, and POW!—it will all be over.* But instead, our driver put the truck in gear; and when the other truck got within fifteen or twenty feet of us, he took off, staying in the lead.

The sun was still pretty high in the sky when we began to notice that we were coming into a populated area. The buildings and houses were more numerous and closer together, and some of the streets we drove on had curbs and gutters. Suddenly, as is the custom in Java, it began to rain. It poured down, just as it had when we were walking along the railroad track the day before. And just as suddenly, it stopped; but the clouds remained.

Now we were passing some sort of commercial area with shops and stores. At times it reminded me of places I'd seen in Manila, but I thought the Dutch influence made it have a more American appearance than the Spanish influence that was predominant in the Philippines. The street we were traveling on was very crowded with vehicular traffic, as well as pedestrian. Japanese army trucks were everywhere, mixed with a variety of small command cars and motorcycles. Just seeing all the pedestrians gave me a sinking feeling to think that it might be a long time before I would be able to walk the streets again—though at that time I had no idea just how long it would really be.

The truck driver wound around on several streets and finally came to a stop in front of a house in the residential part of town. We were ordered to get off the truck and go to the sidewalk in front of the house. As soon as the guards were satisfied that they had all us "round eyes" off the truck, they ordered us to go to one side of the lawn and sit down as close together as we could and face the street. Someone turned to look at the house and caught a fist alongside his head. We were not to look behind us.

The house faced a large park with lots of trees. Near the center was a little playground with swings and seesaws. The park had been taken over by a cavalry outfit, and there were corrals which were designated by ropes tied to stakes that had been driven into the ground. Between the corrals were high stacks of baled hay.

The house we were in front of was some sort of command post. Many people, mostly officers, were continually coming and going. Every once in a while one of them would stop long enough to take our picture. In a way, it was interesting to see the different facial expressions when they realized that there were Americans among the small group sitting on the lawn in front of their headquarters. We were beginning to find that the oriental is not as inscrutable as legend would have one believe. It was easy to discern the individuals who thought we were despicable. The expression on their faces was one of utter disgust. It was a look that couldn't be hidden, though they probably didn't care. Then there was the individual who was curious, who probably hadn't seen many westerners or "round eyes" before. A look of sheer curiosity would show on his face. And a few even gave us looks of compassion. The sympathy they seemed to feel probably was not so much for us as it was for the realization that their government—their country—had made a bad mistake by drawing America into the war. One or two spoke to us, asking us if we were American. But the guard standing nearby growled at them, so there wasn't too much of that.

We were kept in front of the headquarters house for a little more than an hour. Finally, we were ordered to form into a squad and get in the street. Then we were marched several blocks to what we were told later was the governor's mansion. The mansion itself was a very sumptuous and elegant-looking structure. It wasn't hard to tell that it represented government. Along the avenue that ran in front of the mansion was an iron picket fence with a gate at each end. Beyond the gates was a paved drive that circled at the portico and returned to the street. The lawn area between the two strips of paved driveway was covered with a luxurious lawn of deep, green grass. Off to the left were the servants' quarters and storage buildings, nestled among tall mango trees.

We were marched through the gate that was to the right of the property and then directed to the middle of the lawn, about fifty feet from the street. We were ordered to sit down, backs to the street, and not talk among ourselves. As we came through the gate, we saw that we were not the first captives to be brought to this location. There were about twenty-five other guys there, Australian and American, and more were being added to our number continually.

We had been there for perhaps an hour or more when a Japanese sergeant and a couple of privates came up and began to talk to the two soldiers who had been guarding us. After a short conference, the sergeant yelled out some unintelligible words and gestured with his arms. We got the idea that he wanted us to stand up. We stood. More yelling and screaming, and it became apparent that he wanted us in two ranks. We formed two ranks. Then he yelled, *"Bungo!"* Bungo? What was *bungo*? "Awun, two, shree, fo, *Bungo!"*

"I think he wants us to count off," someone said.

The sergeant stepped back a pace or two, looked at us, and again yelled, *"Bungo!"* We began the count, "One, two, three, four, one . . ."

"Bakaroda!" screamed the sergeant. Whaley was the fifth man in line; and because of many months of training in the American method of counting off by squads, he had, as a matter of course, repeated the number "one" to designate the second squad. The sergeant apparently didn't care about squads. He just wanted to know how many captives he had. He could have counted them himself, but, as we would soon learn, there are ways and then there are Japanese ways. He was doing it the Japanese way.

Once again, *"Bungo!"* "One, two, three, four, one . . ."

"Bakaroda!" screamed one of the privates with a rifle as he charged at Whaley and slammed him in the chest with his rifle butt. Not expecting the savage attack, Whaley fell back through the rear rank, knocking me and several others to the ground as he tried to get away from the rifle butt and retain his balance. As

we got to our feet and re-formed the two ranks, someone said, "I think he wants you to say five."

One more time. *"Bungo!"*

"One, two, three, four, FIVE, six. . ." The man on the end of the rank said twenty-five. All told, the Japanese had fifty captives in hand.

After the counting episode we were told to sit down, and again were warned not to talk among ourselves. We watched the traffic coming to the mansion in an endless stream. It didn't seem that the cars that came here were in such a hurry as the ones at the simple headquarters house had been, but the variety of transportation was much the same.

Darkness was hastened by a cloudy sky and a misty rain. Nighttime fell and we had been sitting in the drizzle for about thirty minutes when one of our group began to talk with one of the guards to see if we couldn't be moved to some kind of shelter. There was a small storage building just the other side of the driveway to our left, and through pidgin English and gestures it was suggested that we be allowed to take advantage of a canopy that covered an area in front of this building. The guard indicated that he couldn't do anything; he would see the sergeant. In a few minutes the sergeant came around and the guard presented our request to him. After a little discussion, the sign was that the sergeant would have to check with someone else, an officer, supposedly. In a few minutes the sergeant returned, spoke with the guard, and indicated that we could move to the canopy, but we'd have to do it slowly—no fast moves. We hadn't been under the canopy five minutes when we knew we had made a mistake. The gnats and mosquitoes were eating us up! We asked the guard if we could go back into the rain. We couldn't understand his words, but we did understand his answer: You made the choice; you suffer the consequences.

We suffered the consequences for nearly another hour before the sergeant returned and had another conference with our guards. We had asked for food at the same time we asked to get out of the rain, so we were hoping that this request was being fulfilled. The conference broke up, and the guards, again with much yelling and gesturing, managed to make us understand that we were to form a column four abreast and march out the gate.

It was dark; traffic on the street was using blackout lights; and it was drizzling rain. We were marched to the very center of the street so that we were between two lanes of traffic moving in opposite directions. It didn't take too much imagination to realize that the odds of us getting to our destination—wherever it was—were just about nil. Here we were: We couldn't understand our orders, and we didn't know where we were going. The drivers of the vehicles, for the most part, for sure, were strangers to the streets and could hardly see where they were going, much less see us. Russian roulette grown up! We walked some four blocks, and then by some miracle got through one lane of vehicular traffic to a nice, quiet side street in a residential area. We had gone two or three blocks from the busy avenue when the guards directed us to turn into the driveway of a small bungalow, a single-family residence.

At the end of the driveway was a small garage. It looked like what Americans call a one-and-a-half-car garage. The hinged doors were about half closed. In the space between the edges of the doors, sitting on a chair taken from someone's kitchen, was a Japanese soldier, another guard. The two guards who brought us to this place spoke for a minute with the soldier at the door then indicated that we were to form in a single file and walk into the garage. It was as dark as pitch inside, and a few low whispers told us that we were not the first to be there. I had no idea how many men were there before us; but we did manage to walk around them, as we had been told, to the back wall of the tiny structure.

The first ones in the garage had to place their backs against the rear wall; the next row in front of them placed their backs against the bellies of the row against the wall, and so on until the little building was packed full. Then the order was given, "Sit down!" Common sense tells one that a standing person uses less room than someone sitting down, so we had our problems. It was more than an hour before all the knees had been forced into the proper armpits, feet rested on bellies, and heads in crotches, and we could settle down to await the dawn.

Just as everyone had finally positioned themselves, a voice piped up, breaking the tense silence, "I have to go to the privy." That was when we learned our second word of the Japanese language. After some discussion, we learned that the word the Japanese wanted to hear was "*benjo*." All night long the procession of *benjo* users filed out to a tree in the back yard of the house where the garage was located, did their bit, and filed back into the steaming heat given off by the some 125 bodies in that small garage. I managed to drift off into a light sleep; however, before I could enjoy it, I would be awakened by one of the guys I was interlaced with when he needed to change his position. No one got any real sleep. It was a miserable night.

The sun had risen above the horizon the next morning before the Japanese let us out of the makeshift jail cell. We were told by an English-speaking officer that we were to come out of the garage and go into the back yard and that we would get some food a little later. There were three or four guards to watch us; and while we waited we got into some pretty lively conversations with them. The guards passed out cigarettes and asked our ages, whether or not we were married, and where we lived in America. This bit of interaction went on for thirty minutes or so before the food was brought around. We were surprised to find that our breakfast was going to be big "cathead" biscuits, canned Australian butter, and plum and peach jam— with hot tea to wash it all down. There was plenty of everything, so we were able to fill our stomachs for the first time since our last meal aboard ship on the evening of February 28. This day was March 4, 1942.

As we finished eating, we were taken in groups of ten to the front of the house to be assigned some sort of work detail. I was assigned to a project that consisted of moving an overstuffed chair from one house about a block and a half away to the house next to the one where we had spent the night. The sight up and down the street was something to behold. The neighborhood had the appearance of any American middle-class neighborhood. The houses were on fifty- and sixty-foot lots and sat back some thirty or forty feet from the street, giving them the usual front yard. The houses had detached garages, much like ours in America. But at each house, all the appliances, such as refrigerators and washing machines, as well as much of the furniture including the sofas, mattresses, and upholstered chairs, had been tossed willy-nilly into the front yards. It looked like a disaster area. We passed close enough to look into some of the houses and could see several *tatami* mats on the floors and the Japanese soldiers' kits stacked against the walls. Otherwise, the rooms were empty.

The work detail I had gone on was finished in twenty minutes or so, and we were taken back to the house where we had spent the night. Behind the railing on the front porch, several Japanese officers were sitting in kitchen chairs. Using the top of the porch rail as a counter or makeshift desk, they were recording personal information on each captive. Two lines were formed, one for Australians and one for Americans. Officers were to be first in line, followed by petty officers and then the enlisted men. When I came before the Japanese officer, he asked me the same questions he had asked the others: name, rank and serial number, and the name of my ship. As soon as all of us had been through the questioning routine, we were put in trucks and taken to the Serang city prison. Of course, we hadn't known where we were going until we got there.

9

SERANG CITY PRISON, JAVA

As the driver pulled the truck to a stop in front of the Serang prison gate, I was reminded of the Spanish missions around San Antonio, Texas. The multitude of blank walls must have served to create that impression, because the architectural features of the buildings certainly had no other Spanish influence of any kind. In any case, we unloaded from the truck, formed a column two abreast, and marched through the large main gate.

Immediately on going through the gate, we walked through a sort of tunnel formed by the wall of the office on the right, the wall of the kitchen on the left, and the floor of a storage area overhead. Just beyond this "tunnel" was a large open area. It was a walled courtyard that had a walkway completely around it. We had to go through another gate made of wooden planking to get into the center of the courtyard, where there was a well. There were about one hundred and twenty-five of us assembled in the courtyard, and then thirty to thirty-five at a time were taken away and put in cells which were on three sides of the courtyard. The cells could not be seen because of the ten-foot wall that separated them from the courtyard. There were thirty-five in my cell. The sign above the door indicated that the cell was meant to accommodate seventeen people.

Each cell measured about thirty feet front-to-back and fifteen side-to-side. The only entrance was a door made of iron bars spaced six or seven inches apart with pieces of flat iron dividing the door into four vertical panels. The door was about three feet wide and six feet six inches high. Inside the cell was an aisle about three feet wide that ran from front to back. On each side of the aisle a raised area ran from front to back, except for a small area at the front on the left side that was the same level as a floor of the aisle. The raised portion of the cell served as the bed for the prisoners. It was about six feet wide from aisle to wall. The little area at the front was where the toilet barrel and water keg were kept. Air and light came in at two places. One was the door in front of the wall, the other was a small window about two feet square near the roof in the rear wall. In the center of the cell was a single light bulb hanging down to within ten feet of the floor. The ceiling was arched. The aisle was concrete, as were the raised sleeping platforms.

Our group of thirty-five was taken to a cell on the right side of the jail. We were told that the left side had been reserved for civilian Javanese prisoners. Our first effort would be to find out how much space each man would have. It figured out to a little less than two feet per man, measuring horizontally from front wall to back wall. It didn't take too long to get acquainted with the accommodations since there were only four walls, the ceiling, and the floor/sleeping platforms to see; it could all be seen from any place in the room. Next would be the rules, and these weren't long in coming.

As soon as all prisoners had been assigned spaces, a small Japanese lieutenant came to our door and recited the rules: Everyone must not talk in loud voices. Everyone must stop sleeping between six o'clock in the morning and ten o'clock at night. Everyone will get two meals a day. Everyone will take a bath every ten days. No one can read or smoke. Everyone must obey the Japanese soldiers. So began the first day of our incarceration.

The first week or two in Serang prison was spent marking off the days. Someone had procured a pencil and had drawn a calendar on the wall. We were confident that it would not be more than a couple of weeks before the Dutch would drive the Japanese off Java; then we would all be released and could go home. So the first two weeks were a practice in optimism. Two or three times a day we could hear aircraft overhead, and we would imagine that they were the Dutch. By the time two weeks had gone by, we knew they were the Japanese.

Of course we got no firsthand news, but the second cell over from us held some fifty Dutch and Eurasian civilians including men, women, and children. They were allowed to send money out to purchase food, and every once in a while they would get the latest rumor back to us. These rumors kept us going for a while, but soon it became apparent that somewhere in their midst was an awful optimist. We quit giving their reports much credence.

At any rate, most of our time during those first days in prison was spent talking about food—meals that we'd had in the past. We would take turns telling about dinners or suppers that we had especially enjoyed, describing in fine detail every item that had been included and savoring the memories. That bit of pastime consumed quite a few hours during the first days. Some of the guys even went to the trouble to collect recipes and menus and vowed that they would devote their first days of freedom, weeks even, to trying every one of them. It was here in Serang that I saw for the first time men snarl at one another over a crumb of bread. The scene would be repeated many times before liberation day.

One day we heard that the Dutch had capitulated; we couldn't believe it. (The Dutch capitulated on March 7, 1942.) Then the days began to be long and worrisome, as were the nights. It helped when after about two weeks the rules were relaxed and we were allowed to have smoking tobacco. Some of the fellows had money with them that had not been confiscated or stolen; so we military prisoners were allowed to buy from the outside, but not on the scale that the Dutch and Eurasians could. Tobacco was about the only thing we could get.

By the time we had been in Serang prison three weeks, friendships began to spring up between the guards and prisoners, especially the guards who were on duty during the night. Not all of them were curious about their round-eye prisoners, but there were two or three who, in addition to being curious, were also pretty good politicians. One of them may even have had a humane streak in him. He was a real country bumpkin and could be told anything and he would believe it. We called him Charlie.

Charlie had a desperate desire to learn English. The nights he was on duty, he would spend his whole shift standing outside the cell doors trading Japanese lessons for English lessons. He would give cigarettes to those who could recite some of his Japanese lessons from memory. Charlie was a happy-go-lucky sort of fellow. We never knew how he kept from getting his brains knocked out, because to fraternize with the prisoners was supposed to be strictly taboo. But every night that he was on duty, as soon as his section took over, we could hear Charlie striding across the cobblestones of the courtyard calling, "America! Oy America," and could see the sparks flying from his boots as he scraped them on the stones.

The food we received at Serang jail was, I believe, the worst of my whole POW experience. We were fed twice a day, around six o'clock in the morning and then again around five o'clock in the afternoon. The meal, if it could be called that, consisted of a pint of the filthiest rice imaginable. It contained rocks, weevils, worms (sometimes an inch or more long), rat droppings, and insects of all types. Usually there was a half of a thoroughly rotten sweet potato or a quarter of a boiled duck egg. The drink was weak, but hot, tea.

As a result of this contaminated food, some of us began to have dysentery and diarrhea. Medical services were not provided—no doctors were made available, and no sort of medication was ever offered. We were all on our own as far as health was concerned.

Within the first three weeks, very probably even sooner, we began to devise ways to get around some of the rules. When a man contracted dysentery it was impossible for him to get a decent night's sleep. So we would gather around him during the daytime so the guards couldn't see him and let him get what sleep he could during the day. One day, however, a feisty little lieutenant was making an inspection tour. When he looked into our cell, he saw this group of men all sitting together. He suspected something and ordered them to separate. They continued to stay put, just staring at him. He became quite enraged and began yelling the order for them to disperse. Still no reaction from the prisoners, except to continue to stare at the officer quietly. Suddenly, he unsnapped his holster, drew the little .25-caliber revolver he was carrying, and shouted for the men to disperse. They scattered like frightened quail. Fortunately, they had awakened the sleeping man and he was able to sit up. The Japanese lieutenant never really knew what was happening, although he certainly had his suspicions.

Each time the food was brought around, two men were allowed to carry the toilet barrel out to empty it. That was a chore that was passed around, not because it was so bad, but because those who emptied the "honey bucket" would get to bathe. The bath wasn't a Japanese-sanctioned privilege, but a stolen one. We did manage to get our scheduled bath about every ten days or so, but we got no haircuts or shaves. As a result, it wasn't too long before the eighteen- and twenty-year-olds that went into Serang jail began to look like forty- and fifty-year-old prospectors. The bad food and recurring sickness didn't do much to make the image any better.

One day, for reasons known only to the Japanese, we had a general shake-up of prisoners. Some of us were shifted to different cells, and I ended up with four other men in a cell that had been designed for one. There was only space enough for one person to sleep comfortably, so we would take turns through the night. While one man lay on the cot that was usually folded up against the wall, the other four would try to find a place near the door where they might get a little fresh air. Ours was the only cell that was in the courtyard, and that made it accessible to the guards at all times. This arrangement had its advantages and its disadvantages. In the daytime occupants of that cell were guaranteed not to be able to catch a catnap, as was possible in the cells behind the wall. But at night they could talk to the guards who had a tendency to be friendly and who liked to hand out cigarettes. This was the cell where Charlie spent a lot of his time, giving lessons in Japanese and learning something about America.

I was in this uncomfortable cell for only a few days before there was another shake-up. This time I was moved to the most terrible cell of all. It was a storeroom that had been converted to a cell. It measured about twelve by fifteen feet and there were twelve men in it: eleven survivors of *Perth* and me. When I entered that cell I became a member of the "Dirty Dozen."

I was told that there had always been twelve men in the cell and that I had taken the place of a petty officer who, for some reason or another, had been moved in with the officers who acted as liaisons or representatives for the POWs. These officers had been pressing since the day we arrived to get medical care, better food, and more frequent baths.

The room to which I had been moved had no facilities at all to accommodate prisoners. There were just four walls, the ceiling, and the floor. The floor was concrete and had not been cleaned of the filth that had accumulated while the room was used as a storeroom, making it impossible to keep our bodies even reasonably clean. The conditions were aggravated by the lack of ventilation. The door was solid wood and the one window was nearly out of reach, with a fixed sash that could not be opened. When one man would stand on another man's shoulders, he could see through the lower pane; however, he couldn't reach the top of the sash to loosen it so we could pull it out of the frame.

Not one of the Dirty Dozen had any sort of bedding. We had only the very sparse bit of fat on our bones to act as a cushion on the hard concrete floor. All of us developed sores on our hips and elbows as a result of the constant scraping and rubbing on the concrete. I think the only reason the sores didn't cover us completely was because we would pack them with salt every chance we got.

I had been a member of the Dirty Dozen only a few days when a call came to the prison for a work detail. Because our conditions were so terrible, the officers, our liaisons, suggested that the men in our cell be the ones to go on the detail. It was an exciting moment when we, all twelve of us, were taken out of the cell. We had two guards with us as we walked a couple of miles or so to a golf course somewhere on the edge of town. Our job was to unload drums of aviation gasoline from trucks and arrange them in rows on the fairways of the golf course. We left for the work site about ten o'clock in the morning and worked until noon. Our noon meal came from a Japanese kitchen and was the best food we had tasted since we'd been in Serang. We finished work about four in the afternoon.

On the way back to the jail one day, an old Javanese man with a load of bananas crossed the street in front of us. On an impulse, our guard asked us if we would like to have some bananas. We answered that we surely would, so he stopped the old man. Each of us was given a handful of bananas, about five or six, and the guard handed the vendor a paper bill. It was a Japanese occupation guilder. The old man looked at it and refused to take it. He wouldn't even touch it. The guard argued with him in Malay for a few minutes, but the old man remained adamant about the money. He wanted a real Dutch guilder. All of a sudden, the guard swung his rifle butt into the old man's ribs and knocked the breath out of him. He lay on the ground and gasped for breath for a few minutes while we and some Javanese who had gathered as the argument got louder looked on. Not one of the civilians made any move to intervene, because the second guard stood with his rifle at the ready position. As soon as the old man had recovered his breath, he reached up and accepted the phony money. As we resumed our walk back to the jail, we all felt very sorry for the old man but felt there was no realistic way we could have helped.

After three or four weeks, our officers finally convinced the Japanese commandant that we could prepare our own food and furthermore that we should be allowed to do just that. The jail kitchen had no oven, and the Japanese agreed to get the necessary materials for us to build one. A couple of bricklayers were found among the prisoners, and the Japanese brought in sand, cement, and brick. They also agreed to supply tin so we could make the pans needed to bake our bread. Tin-snips and hammers were provided, along with a hundred five-gallon kerosene cans to be used in making the pans. They furnished yeast and flour and actually brought in logs that the prisoners could cut up for firewood. One of the Aussie sailors had been a tinsmith, so he was given the job of making the bread pans. Luckily, I was chosen to be his helper. This job gave us the opportunity to get out of the stinking cell for about eight hours a day. Things were beginning to look up.

It took nearly a week to construct the oven. In the meantime, we bread pan makers had turned out some fifty or so pans. The baker had been provided with washtubs in which to mix the dough, and we were on our way. We had baked bread in the new oven only twice before we got the word that we were being transferred to Batavia.

The announcement that we would be moved again was made in what we were to learn was typical Japanese fashion: on the spur of the moment or at the very last minute. One morning shortly after we finished what was meant to be breakfast, we were told that in an hour we would be loaded into trucks and taken to a beautiful camp where we would have room to walk around, take baths—all the amenities we didn't have at Serang. It was not without some misgivings, but with an awful lot of hope, that we boarded the trucks in front of the jail shortly before noon amid much shouting and yelling. It seemed the Japanese could never conduct an operation with shouting and yelling. It took almost half an hour to get the eight trucks loaded, and we were relieved when the signal was finally given for the lead truck to pull out.

As we rode along the streets of Serang, the civilians stared at us, some with scorn, others with fingers forming a "V," their hands held low to hide the victory sign from the Japanese guards. Soon we were out of Serang and back on a road running between the rice paddies. Dust stirred up by the trucks ahead of us filled the air. We passed several villages, and at each one there were crowds of very young children standing along the side of the road waving Japanese flags and cheering as the trucks sped past. To satisfy our own feelings, we shouted back at them. I felt sure they neither understood nor cared what we said, but it made us feel better.

10

BICYCLE CAMP, BATAVIA

The drive from Serang took about three hours, so it was midafternoon when we pulled up in front of the encampment that was to become known to us as the Bicycle Camp. We were impressed immediately with the large shade trees that the trucks parked under along the street. We were ordered to unload and stand beside our truck to be counted. After two or three recounts and much comparing of notes, the guards and their commander agreed that they had arrived in Batavia with the same number of prisoners they had counted when we left Serang. All this, despite the fact that we had not stopped anywhere along the way. Then we were marched into the camp—the Aussies called it a compound—and were astounded at what we found inside. We were assigned to a regular barracks, and directly across an open area was another barracks filled with troops of an American artillery outfit. We'd had no idea that there were any other American military on Java.

Our first few days were spent just accepting this heaven. The barracks were made of stucco-covered brick with the inevitable red tile roof. Each of the buildings was about two hundred feet long and about thirty feet wide. On each end were two rooms made private by high walls that reached the ceiling. Each wall had a door. Running the length of the building was a three-foot-wide corridor with open cubicles on each side. The cubicles were formed by partitions which were about seven feet tall and seven feet wide. There was no ceiling over these open-air bins, so one could see the bottom sides of the tiles on the roof. Verandas ran the length of the front and back sides between the ells formed by the two-room arrangements on each end of the structure.

In peacetime, we learned, the Bicycle Camp had been occupied by a Dutch army infantry unit who were provisioned with bicycles, thus the name Bicycle Camp. This camp was located in a predominantly residential neighborhood, which seemed a little strange to me. I supposed that the location was necessitated by a lack of available space on an island that had to use most of its land to grow food. The camp was situated between what seemed to be two main thoroughfares, making the compound some eight or nine hundred feet from front to back. In the middle of the camp was a twenty-foot road that ran straight through from one thoroughfare to the other. And on the right side of the camp road, as one entered what we came to know as the front gate and which faced south, was the officers' quarters. The American army officers and a few Dutch army officers occupied the quarters during the time the compound was used as a prisoner-of-war camp.

Beyond the officers' quarters was the first of five barracks. Each barracks was separated by an open area measuring about one hundred feet from barracks to barracks. Past the fifth barracks building, with its back facing the other thoroughfare, was a storeroom. The space between the east end of the barracks and the perimeter of the camp held washrooms and laundry facilities with a wide area of fifty feet or so separating the end of the barracks from these facilities. On the left side of the camp road, immediately inside the gate, was a small building that served as quarters for the guards, both Dutch and Japanese. Behind the guardhouse was the kitchen, which measured about forty feet by forty feet and which had a tile floor, stoves, cooking pots, and all the other equipment necessary to make it an efficient place to prepare food. Then past the guardhouse was another series of five barracks. One was used as a hospital; the rest were assigned to Australian and British troops.

We survivors from *Houston* and *Perth* were the last prisoners of war to be brought into Bicycle Camp, and things began to become pretty well organized. However, because the field artillery unit, as well as some Aussie soldiers, had gotten there before us, all the officers' quarters were taken; so *Houston*'s officers had a small cottage just at the end of the barracks we enlisted men had been assigned to.

During those first few days of adjustment to our new surroundings, the soldiers of the 131st Field Artillery began to take care of the *Houston* survivors' lack of clothing and shoes. The 131st was a Texas National Guard unit that had been mobilized in 1941, and the majority of its members were from Texas.

Being a Texan myself, I was interested to know if there might be some among them that I might know. I found no one I knew, but I heard that one fellow in Service Battery was from Marlin, Texas. His name, I was told, was Otho Casey. I had an uncle who lived in Marlin, and he had married a Casey. I had visited Uncle Hubert and his family when I was young and growing up, but I had never met any of his wife's relatives. So I looked up this fellow Texan to see if he knew my Uncle Hubert. I went over to the 131st barracks and began to ask where I could find one Otho Casey. After asking several of the guys, I was finally directed to his cubicle. I went in and introduced myself and began to describe my Uncle Hubert and his family. I told Otho that my uncle was a barber who'd had a shop in Marlin for a number of years, how many kids he and his wife Nettie had, and a few other things that I could think of. As I spoke, a rather amused expression began to gather on Otho's face; and when I had told all that I knew of Uncle Hubert and his family, Otho said, "That's my aunt and uncle, too. My daddy's sister married your Uncle Hubert." We both agreed that it was indeed a small world.

When the Dutch army had capitulated, the 131st was somewhere near central Java. The Japanese had taken all their trucks and guns, what they could find of them, but had let them keep all their personal belongings. (Also, they had been allowed to keep the battalion funds—one million dollars in cash, according to rumor.) After it was discovered we had common kin, almost to the point of being kinfolks ourselves, Otho gave me a shelter half, a pair of boots, a blanket, and a couple of khaki shirts and pants—items that took care of my clothing needs for a good while.

For a few days we were kept busy arranging our cubicles to make them livable. I was in a cubicle with Claude W. Washburn and Claude Parker. Washburn and I had met at the recruiting station in Houston, Texas, and we had gone through boot camp together in San Diego, California. We had both requested USS *Houston* as our first choice as a duty station and had been assigned to her in early April, just after we returned from boot leave. And we had both been assigned to the 4th Division, a deck division, when we reported aboard, so we developed a pretty strong friendship. We had made nearly all our liberties together while the ship was in the Philippines. We were almost as close as brothers. Washburn had been taken captive earlier than I had, at a different place on the beach, and had spent his first six weeks as a prisoner of war in a movie theater in Serang—a real hell-hole of a place. He was fortunate to have survived that experience.

We collected bamboo from some source to build our beds. Washburn and Parker built their beds against each partition, and I laid some bamboo poles across the tops of the partition, next to the corridor, and laced them with strands of rope that some Aussies had stolen from the Japanese. We got a couple of orange crates and made them into a cabinet of sorts, and we were in the housekeeping business.

Those first days went by rapidly because our lives had been thoroughly reversed as compared to what we had been through the preceding six weeks in Serang. It seemed that there was something new to learn every day. One of our first lessons regarded camp discipline. We were told that we must obey all orders given by the Japanese soldiers; we must salute all Japanese soldiers; and we must not try to escape. These orders took a little getting used to, and there was a fair amount of slapping around and bashing with rifle butts before we became thoroughly indoctrinated.

We hadn't been in Bicycle Camp very long before our officers, both army and navy, told us that military courtesy was going to be done away with for the duration of our incarceration, because they felt we were all in the same boat and that all the saluting and saying "sir" had no real significance.

Somehow we had managed, up to this point, to maintain the tendency we'd had in the first weeks of our captivity to be optimistic about our future. During that time we had the feeling that within a matter of weeks—at the most a couple of months— we would either be set free or liberated by American forces. In Bicycle Camp we learned the bitter truth, for among the many things the 131st brought into camp with them was a radio.

The existence of the radio, though it was fairly common knowledge among the Americans in Bicycle Camp, was kept a virtual secret. Only two or three of the army officers knew where it was, and only they listened to it. Later what news they heard was passed around camp by word of mouth. This, of course, was a source of many wild rumors and raised false hopes many times. There was also a map in the camp—a page out of an atlas that someone had procured from some unknown place. The map was kept up to date as well as possible in connection with the radio news; and if a man was lucky, he could see it every once in a while. Seeing the map was a perspective to the news, but it certainly didn't do anything to promote or sustain optimism. From time to time I was among those privileged to see the map. Afterward, we would sit around and try to determine the strategy behind certain moves of American forces in the South Pacific. From the news we received during the time we were in Bicycle Camp in Batavia, it was easy to see that our situation was just on the borderline between weak and completely hopeless. But for some strange reason, we never really lost the hope and the feeling that, in the end, America would be victorious and that we would get back home again.

The Japanese, of course, were not completely stupid; they knew there was a radio in camp and they made every effort to find it. They held numerous searches, some lasting for several hours as they went through everyone's personal belongings trying to uncover the forbidden item. More than a few severe beatings were suffered by the officers who had knowledge of the radio, but none ever broke and revealed its location.

The state of euphoria that had been created when we arrived at Bicycle Camp lasted for nearly two weeks. We stayed busy, both mentally and physically, getting to know the men of the 131st, and savoring the expanded freedom to move about, which—when compared to our jail cells in Serang—seemed to include the whole outdoors. Also, there were several hundred Australians in the camp, so much time was spent getting acquainted with them and swapping stories about life in our respective countries. In addition, we were busy collecting items to make our living quarters more livable and convenient. In short, our time was our own. We had only a few required duties which didn't require a lot of time. Mostly they were annoying, like lining up to be counted twice a day and being watchful for any roving Japanese guard so that the required "*Kioski!*" (attention), "*Kari!*" (salute), "*Yasemae!*" (at ease) could be addressed as he approached. Failure to be alert usually meant a "massage" with a rifle butt. And if the guard felt energetic, he might resort to including the hob-nails of his boots or a bamboo pole. The massage was an unpleasant experience regardless of method or equipment used, so everyone developed an acute sense of awareness for Japanese guards. In just a short while, after a few of the men had been left with bloody heads and bodies, we developed a sort of "civil defense" system. As soon as it was discovered that a guard had entered a barracks, a runner would be sent to warn the adjoining barracks so that men sleeping or otherwise goofing off would be alerted and be ready to render the proper honors when the representative of Hirohito and Dai Nippon arrived in their vicinity.

Boredom was beginning to set in, when it was announced that all prisoners were going to be given the opportunity to work outside the camp. One afternoon everyone was called to parade formation, which means to form up to be counted, so the Japanese could look us over and select the ones who appeared to be healthy and able to work. Those selected would be sent out on working details the next day. This bit of news caused quite a bit of excitement, and nearly everyone was eager to go. Of course, there were doubts and trepidation, but at least it was worth a try. I was among the hundred or so that were selected.

The next morning we were sent out of camp in groups of twenty-five or thirty to go on work details. We had been told to take a lunch with us, since the work would last all day. The kitchen had prepared lunches for everyone.

Just after roll call, we were marched to the front gate and

put on one of the several trucks waiting there. As usual, the Japanese method of much shouting and scurrying between trucks was carried out by the guards. Finally, after some three or four recounts, comparing of notes on clipboards, lustily shouted "*Hais!*" as the sergeants saluted the officer in charge, and explicit commands given to the drivers of the trucks, we were on our way.

It was a thrilling but somewhat heartbreaking experience to ride down the street and see people doing ordinary everyday chores in relative freedom. It was a luxury we could only dream of. I felt sure that there was a certain amount of envy in everyone's mind as we drove to our work site that day, and the succeeding days as well. We had now been prisoners of war for about two months.

The work detail that I and my shipmates had been assigned to was in the port area of Batavia, an area called Tanjong Priok. Here were the docks and piers for the seagoing merchant ships to moor to and warehouses for storing the goods and refineries of British Petroleum Limited. Our job was at one of the refining facilities.

When the Japanese invaded and captured Hong Kong, it was easy to see that their rapid advance was going to land them in the Netherlands East Indies before too long. At that time, the Dutch began operation of their "scorched earth" policy, a practice that they had used in Europe when the German invasion and occupation of Holland was imminent. The British Petroleum Limited refinery was a victim of that policy. The whole facility had been set on fire and had been pretty well destroyed, with two exceptions. There was one 50,000-barrel storage tank filled with aviation fuel and one 50,000-barrel storage tank filled with diesel fuel that had not been completely burned. It was evident that the diesel fuel had been set afire; about half of it was burned. The aviation fuel storage tank had caught fire, too, but had not exploded. About half of the gasoline was still in the tank; only the vapors from the hot fuel had burned. Our job was to put the remaining products in large barrels and store them off to one side, where trucks would pick them up later.

Someone, the Japanese I supposed, had rigged up piping and valves which allowed the diesel and aviation gas to be put in the barrels from a station on the ground some two hundred feet or so from the tanks. There, in the shade of a little lean-to shack, was a valve and hose arrangement that could be used to put the fuel in the barrels. The barrels themselves were much larger than the ordinary fifty-five-gallon barrel one sees in America. Someone told us that they were two-hundred-liter barrels, but we didn't know for sure that was what they were. All I knew was they were *big* and hard to roll on the soft, sandy soil where we had to handle them.

The soldier in charge of our detail was a skinny little shrimp of a guy by the name of Ikeda. He had a keen sense of humor and wasn't a slave driver. Rather than work, he would much sooner be playing a practical joke on someone. We spent a good deal of our time doing just that. I often wondered how he managed to live in an army that, by all appearances, had such strict rules of discipline. He, as opposed to the attitude of all other soldiers we came in contact with, didn't give a damn about conquering America, Britain, or any of the so-called allies. At least that was the attitude he displayed before us. He would much rather talk—with gestures, pictures, and pidgin English, for he could neither speak nor understand English—about one's home life and family than about war and armies and airplanes. He always had a couple of pots of hot tea and a big basket of tea cakes when we arrived for work in the mornings. He would wait until the trucks and the guards from the camp were gone before he would bring them out; but bring them out he did, every morning. While we relaxed in the shade, he would engage one or two guys in a conversation about their homes and families. He had some pictures that showed him as a civilian with long hair, standing beside a big, shiny automobile. He was proud of the car and wanted to get back to it as soon as possible.

Although Ikeda would usually change the subject if it seemed headed toward armies, navies, and war, one day he did become engaged in a discussion about bravery. It was proposed that an Australian or an American would be braver than a Japanese soldier. Now, this was a challenge to Ikeda, and he debated the subject for quite some time, never in anger but in a determined way. Finally, one of the Australians taking part in the discussion said that if Japanese soldiers were really so brave he, Ikeda, would let an Australian soldier, the one speaking, take a shot at him with his own rifle as he, Ikeda, ran away from the soldier with the rifle. Ikeda refused right away; he wanted no part of such foolishness. So the Aussie told him to take the rifle and try to shoot him as he ran. Ikeda wouldn't go for that either. It was finally decided that each race had its brave men. But the Aussie would still tease Ikeda, to an annoying degree, most of us thought, about being afraid to run and let someone shoot at him.

The job at the refinery lasted several weeks, then we would be taken to a new site almost every day. One day we were taken to a fuel storage shed near Tanjong Priok. It was just a little native-like shack that had been stacked full of five-gallon cans of gasoline. To get the cans to the truck, we formed a sort of "bucket-brigade" line. The two men unstacking the cans in the shack were Aussies. One would pick up a can and the other would strike it on the bottom with a rock. Sometimes it would cause a hole, other times not; but they were doing the best they could. These weak efforts to sabotage the Japanese operation may have had no effect whatsoever, but our spirits were always raised by even the smallest measure of retaliation. By the time the truck was loaded, it was standing in a pool of gasoline, and we were afraid it was going to explode. Fortunately, it didn't. I don't think the Japanese ever suspected a thing. They just complained about the poor quality of Dutch-made cans.

Another day we were taken to an area that in peacetime had been a public park. The garrison of Japanese stationed in Batavia were now using the park for a parade ground. We were taken out there to police the grounds after the Japanese had held their morning roll call parade. We had been given some demeaning assignments before, but to have to pick up trash and clean up the mess that had been made by Japanese soldiers seemed the lowest form of degradation. We were called upon to do that particular chore only once, for which we were thankful.

Earlier that morning as we had waited off to one side for the Japanese to finish with their ceremonies, we saw a Dutch woman with two children walking along the sidewalk around a flower bed. She was nowhere near the Japanese formation, but our guard took it upon himself to tell her to leave, or maybe he was just following orders. In any event, he had spoken to the woman a couple of times and she had ignored him. The guard became irate and suddenly rushed over to her, jabbing her in the side with his rifle butt and knocking her into the street. The two children, one about three, the other about five, began to scream in fright as they saw their mother go sprawling across the street. The guard went over to them and gave each a hard slap, then shoved them toward their mother, who was getting up off the pavement. Those of us who had seen this incident talked about it later. We thought it had been cowardly on our part to let this incident take place without putting up some kind of opposition; however, at the time our feelings toward the Dutch weren't the best, so we tried to dismiss it from our minds. Even so, there were times when some of us who had been present thought back on the incident and felt just a twinge of regret at not having made some sort of move to defend the woman and her children.

We had arrived in Bicycle Camp about April 18, and all during the months of May and June we had been trying to get accustomed to our new way of life. Certainly, we regretted and resented the fact that we were prisoners of war, but it was a fact we had to face. It was a situation that called upon us to do the best we could with what we had. And about all we had was the life in our bodies. The Japanese, on the other hand, had the guns and therefore controlled just about everything we could do with that fragile life.

Eventually, life in general had settled down into an almost humdrum routine. A little excitement could be expected in the evenings when the work details came back to camp. There were always stories of what had been seen along the streets, of kindness extended by some of the guards, and of the brutal behavior of others. And nearly every day there was something new to buy or trade for, because the more adventurous ones would find a supply of "rare" food like canned sardines or canned fruit of some kind. One time a good supply of Johnny Walker Red Label and Johnny Walker Black Label scotch whiskey and Bols gin came into camp when one of the work details unloaded the holds of a couple of merchant ships that had been scuttled at the piers of Tanjong Priok. The whiskey and gin were going at twenty-five dollars a bottle. And some mighty wild sea stories got told during some of the evening sessions when those most-desired liquids were present. Another time one of the details was used to move stores out of some partly burned warehouses. This job produced a flood of caramelized sweetened condensed milk. Cases of the milk had been exposed to the heat of the fire but had not actually burned. Many a sweet tooth was satisfied for five dollars a can.

Then there were days when these entrepreneurs got caught by the camp guards as they came into camp with their loot. Those were unhappy times and helped to explain the high price of commodities. For to get caught with any of the contraband was to be punished with pain just short of death. The punishment varied and depended on the mood of the persons administering it. None of it was easy to endure. One time it might be the splintering of several large bamboo poles over the offender's head. This punishment could be, and usually was, extended over a period of several hours and left the receiver of such punishment just a few breaths away from death—with bloody head and shoulders, bruised back and legs. Once three to five Japanese guards started beating on a person, they played no favorites with regard to parts of the body. Every part that could be reached was given its share of abuse. This was a noisy procedure. Some of the time the punishment would be more silent, like putting a bamboo pole about two inches in diameter behind a man's knees and having him squat, staying on tiptoe, and then bashing him every time he tilted forward or fell backwards. This procedure, too, produced bloody heads and shoulders; but its worst pain came from the "broken-knee" effect—the result of having to endure not less than eight hours of the bamboo behind the knees to periods of as long as thirty-six hours, without sleep or food. A little water would be given at the necessary intervals to make sure the man being punished would remain conscious.

These were but two of an endless number of tortures inflicted on prisoners of war who were held by the Japanese in camps from Japan itself to the Philippines, Hong Kong, Borneo, Java, Malaya, Burma, and Thailand—indeed, all over East Asia.

But then there were some pleasant times, too—in the beginning. As life began to settle down, as we learned to become prisoners of war, as the Japanese planned what to do with all this free labor for which their manuals of war had no provisions, we began to become a macro-community. We had all the elements of the various societies and cultures we had come from. Everyone had something to contribute. We asked for and were given permission to have educational classes that included such subjects as architecture, literature, the Malay language, the Chinese language, and music. Lectures were given on every conceivable subject—engineering, gold mining, bird watching, law, theater production, anything that it was felt a person had experience in and a lot with leaders who had no experience in anything. A library was started with books that the men had in their kit bags or had picked up on work details. A happy hour was allowed one night a week, and some rousing productions were put on that offered all the entertainment that any peacetime show might have. We even had band concerts when the Japanese contacted local Red Cross people in Batavia and procured musical instruments.

Basketball tournaments were instituted, and it was the Aussies against the Yanks on several occasions. Most Australians had never seen basketball before, much less played a game. Nevertheless, they were fast learners and offered stiff competition in the playoffs. At one stage there were volleyball tournaments that pitted the prisoners against the Japanese guards. That was a wild time. And one time a softball game was played between the Yanks and the Japanese, but that didn't become a regular occurrence. All sorts of handicrafts were practiced. One enterprising Australian cut large pieces of metal from the doors, hoods, and trunks of the three or four automobiles that had been left in the camp when the Dutch evacuated it and went into the frying pan business at ten to fifteen dollars a pan. An eight-inch pan would cost the purchaser ten dollars; the twelve-incher was fifteen dollars. I managed to make spending money by taking up the barber trade: one dollar for the hair, one dollar for the beard, using hand clippers. A shave was two dollars, head or face.

After some time, the Japanese had been persuaded to let the Yanks send a buyer into town and purchase food to supplement the camp food. For a while we were having fresh fruits and vegetables every day. Bacon and eggs for breakfast, while not the usual fare, was enjoyed on a couple of occasions. And our evening meals were tasty, nutritious, and filling. Nearly everyone was gaining weight. Then the end came.

On the Fourth of July, 1942, the work details were sent out as usual. Every one of the Americans was looking forward to the evening meal. It had been the subject of conversation for more than a week. On the Fourth of July the Yanks were going to have steaks for supper. Steaks with all the trimmings. T-bone or sirloin, it made no difference, they were going to be good and they were going to be *big*.

Everything seemed to be fairly routine. Then just minutes after the hustle-bustle of sending the work details out, a call was given for everyone in camp to fall in on parade. As soon as everyone was in place, the Japanese commandant presented to our officers a pledge that he said must be signed by every prisoner of war. The pledge was in essence a promise that the signer would not try to escape and would recognize the Japanese army and its officers and men as his ruling authority. Plainly, the signer would be promising to become a citizen of Japan, subject to the rules and regulations of that country's armed forces. The answer from our officers was a resounding "NO! We will not sign nor will we ask any of our men to sign such a pledge. It's illegal and against all rules of war. NO!" At that point the officers were taken out of camp, leaving only an Australian sergeant major as the senior rank present. The Japanese asked him to sign the pledge and to order the men to sign. He refused. He was severely bashed around, even to the point of unconsciousness, but he steadfastly refused to sign. All the while the rest of the men were being made to stand at attention in the hot sun. It was getting hotter by the minute and men began to pass out. When a man went to the ground the guards would come to him, kick him around until he could stand again, and put him back on his feet. This treatment went on all day. No one was allowed to get a drink of water or to have food or to rest in any manner.

Finally, about the usual time in the afternoon, the work details began to return to camp. As they came through the gate they were greeted by the sight of all their mates lined up in the main road that ran through the camp—looking as though they were going to give up and die at any moment. The returning men were added to the lines and told to stand at attention. None of them knew what was taking place, and no one could tell them because any who dared to speak knew they would be bashed with rifle butts and bamboo poles some of the guards were carrying. In a few minutes the commandant came out and in very broken English tried to tell us what was at issue. He told us the officers had very foolishly advised the men not to sign. All was confusion. The newly arrived men had no idea of the real state of things and could only guess at what to do. Finally, after some thirty minutes or so after the work detail men had arrived in camp, word came from the officers for everyone to sign. If it was made an issue after the war, we could claim duress and unnecessary force had been used to get the signatures. At that word, everyone filed past a desk and signed a copy of the pledge. By dark the commandant had all the men in the camp signed up. That incident changed everything.

The big supper the Yanks had planned was called off. The men got the meat but very few trimmings, and the atmosphere the meal was served in was not conducive to happiness. We all ate a very bitter meal that night.

The guards were doubled, and every man was restricted to the barracks to which he was assigned. There could be no more visiting between barracks. Beginning the next day all food was prepared in one kitchen, and each barracks had to send a party of just enough men to carry the food back to their barracks. That went on for a week. Finally, the Japanese relented enough to let the Americans have their cookhouse back again, but outside buying was no longer allowed. All the food we got from that time on was what the enemy supplied, which was not sufficient to keep up our health.

Some of the privileges were restored, but the spirit of the camp was never the same after the Fourth of July episode. We were always looking for a sudden blitz of some kind and for privileges to be taken away without, from our point of view, any just cause. But then, we were just prisoners of war.

On October 2, 1942, out of the blue, we were called on parade and given notice that 191 Americans were going to be sent out of the camp to an undisclosed destination. They had only three hours to get ready, which really was not such a rush considering they had nothing to prepare. The men selected packed and left with their shipmates and buddies wishing them the best and wondering if they would ever see them again.

11

CHANGI CAMP, SINGAPORE

On October 11, nine days later, the rest of the Americans got a notice that they were to prepare to leave Bicycle Camp. Only those too sick to survive the move and those left to look after them were to be excepted.

It was very early in the morning when we walked out the gate of Bicycle Camp. We hadn't gone half a mile when I began to have trouble with my gear. All I had weighed no more than thirty or forty pounds, and I had tried to devise a way to pack it so it could be transported comfortably. Being a sailor, I had tried to do it navy style. I had folded the few articles of clothing I had and then laid the miscellaneous items such as a book or two, some canned sardines, and a can I used for an oil lamp on top of them and tied the whole mess up as we had been taught to lace up our sea bags and hammocks. It worked fine until I had to shift my belongings on my shoulders a couple of times. Then the rope I had tied around the bundle slipped and I was in trouble. We got on a train bound for Tanjong Priok, and during this ride I got things under control again.

It was daylight when we reached Tanjong Priok. We were taken out to one of the piers where, amid the usual shouting and general confusion, we were put aboard a barge and taken to a ship in the harbor. The *Dai Nichi*, a Japanese troop ship, had been outfitted to accommodate the smaller stature of the Japanese, so the larger-framed Americans had trouble getting settled into the holds. The accommodations in the holds consisted of platforms stacked four high with a space of about two feet between the layers. The platforms were only long enough for a five-foot man to stretch out. Four men could get on one platform, but they were very cramped; and the first ones in had to crawl over the man to the outside to get out. I was lucky. I didn't get one of the platform bunks. I was put in the center of the hold, where all traffic from any direction in the hold had to pass. I was about six feet away from the foot of the ladder, so there was a constant movement going by at all times. This space had one advantage. If and when any air—fresh or otherwise—got down that far, I got some of it. We were four decks below main deck.

We were loaded aboard in the morning, and it was some five or six hours before we got under way. The heat was terrific, as were the odors of the sweaty men. We were fed twice a day and were allowed to go to the *benjo* whenever we could get to the top of the ladder, one at a time. During the five-day trip many of the guys got sick with dysentery, and that added to the disagreeable conditions and odors that were becoming almost overpowering. If people weren't going by to get food, they were trying to get up to go to the latrine. Once in a while a man would get only part way up the ladder before his bowels would loosen. It was a miserable trip, to say the least. Our destination was never told; we just had to guess where we were going. Some of the Aussies said it looked as if we were headed for Singapore. And after five wretched days, that was where we ended up.

We spent two miserable hours in the hot sun and were finally loaded on a barge and taken ashore, where we were immediately loaded on trucks and hauled out to our new home. Changi Village was on the north side of Johore Strait, which separated Singapore and Malaya, and before we left this camp we saw some severely damaged Japanese warships on their way to the naval base at Singapore.

We Americans wound up in an area known as Kitchener Barracks. This area consisted of several barracks buildings, with separate housing for officers. We were in one of the barracks, and some of the Gordon Highlanders were in another just around a small hill. Our barracks was a two-story reinforced concrete structure that sat on a high spot overlooking Johore Strait, a really scenic location. The floors were made of concrete that apparently had been polished many times, for even when we got there they still gleamed like glass. The barracks measured about fifty feet from end to end and was probably about thirty feet or so wide. There were verandas on the front and back with four doors along the walls. I put my bedding on the first floor in about the center of the building—literally on the floor because there was no type of furniture in the building when we moved in.

The officers were housed in what had been the officers' quarters when the large camp had been a British garrison. The quarters had five or six apartment-like flats that were on two floors, with living room and kitchen on the lower floor and bedroom and bath on the second floor. The odd thing to me was that the building was located below the enlisted men's barracks, and the officers had to climb a hill in order to join the men. Knowing of the British stress of class, that was something I never understood. Nonetheless, at one place I knew of, the British officers were "below" the men they commanded.

One of the first differences we were made aware of, as compared to Bicycle Camp, was that the British were responsible for the number count each day. We seldom saw a Japanese guard. Once in a while we could see a pair walking the perimeter of the camp, but I knew of only one time that they actually came into the barracks. Most of the business of the camp was administered by the British, and that was bad for the Americans.

British officers rationed out the food supplies and always managed to cut the Americans short. We had no recourse because all channels of communication were dominated by the British. They labored under the illusion that they still owned the garrison. This was demonstrated when they tried to arrest some Americans who were knocking coconuts out of a tree near their barracks. They maintained the police force in the camp and would even put our guys in jail for acts considered illegal by the Japanese provost marshal and his gang of thieves.

For example, all cooking had to be done on wood fires and firewood was worth its weight in gold—almost. It was very scarce. On certain days firewood was allotted to different groups. We hadn't been in Kitchner Barracks too long when one day we went down to get our ration of firewood. When it was loaded on the trailer, we thought it was a smaller amount than had been given to some British groups ahead of us. The officer accompanying us mentioned that he thought we had been short-changed. The Britisher in charge told him that was all we had coming, and that was that.

The next morning several of us got together and decided that we would find some firewood. We went down in the area where the provost marshal's office was. The "fire truck" was also down in that area. The fire truck was really a water tank with a hand-operated pump and some hose on it that had to be pulled to the area in need. It was stored in a shed that had some big wooden doors. We thought the doors would make fine firewood; all we had to do was get them unhinged and carried to our barracks about a quarter of a mile up the hill. So that night we got what tools we needed and went to the fire-shed. We worked very quietly, and in about fifteen minutes we had the doors lying on the ground. In another fifteen minutes or so we had them at the barracks and began taking them apart. As soon as we had all the planks off the doors, we carried them up to the attic and stored them. We knew there would be a search on for them the next day.

Sure enough, just before sunup the next morning there was a commotion in the kitchen, which was just behind the barracks. The provost marshal himself and one of his MPs were in there questioning the cook about where he had gotten the firewood he was using. The firewood the cook was using at the time had been legally procured, and that was proved soon enough. But the provost marshal just knew that it had been Yanks who had stolen the fire-shed doors. He asked that an American officer be brought up to the kitchen, where he, the provost marshal, would conduct an investigation. Captain Parker was summoned. He came up the hill bleary-eyed and asked what the trouble was. The provost marshal told him his story and asked if the Yanks could be put on parade. The captain agreed to that. In short order everyone was called out on parade and questioned about the doors, but there was no clue as to who did it or where the doors were. For the next week, we brought them out of the attic two or three planks at a time and chopped them up and burned them right along with the legal wood. In the meantime we had continued our search for firewood.

One morning three or four days after the fire-shed doors escapade, we went into an area of the camp we hadn't been in before. We came up on a barbed wire fence that had a sign on it indicating that the area was off limits. That made us curious, so we went over the fence to find out why it should be off limits. We weren't long in finding out. We discovered eight empty wooden barracks. They looked as though they had never been used and were complete with all the walls, floors, and ceiling in place. Doors were hanging in all the rooms, of which there were quite a few. After we had wandered around for a while, we knew that we had discovered a private wood supply. Every night for the rest of the time we were at Kitchner Barracks, five or six of us would go over and rip out an armload each and carry it over to our kitchen. We would miss a night or two every now and then because we would have other chores; but every free night we had, we got the wood. We had just about gutted those temporary barracks by the time we left.

We had been in Singapore about a month when Thanksgiving Day 1942 came around. There was no turkey on the menu, so we thought we ought to have a bird of some kind for Thanksgiving dinner. On another hill just across a little draw from our barracks was the quarters of the high-ranking British officers—brigadier generals, lieutenant generals, and the like. They were the only people allowed to keep or raise any kind of animals for food, and they all had chickens or ducks. One day we had made a trip over in that vicinity and noticed that one pen held some mighty healthy-looking chickens. We decided then and there that chicken would be a good bird to have for our Thanksgiving dinner.

That night after everyone had gotten fairly quiet, we went down into the hollow and walked through the weeds. In peacetime the area no doubt had been well kept, but now weeds had pretty well taken over. We made a little noise as we walked through the weeds, but not enough for anybody at the barracks to hear us. Nevertheless, suddenly there were whistles blowing and flashlights being shined all around. We ducked into the weeds and dodged MPs for about an hour. When they finally gave up and went away, we sneaked back to our barracks. We had no idea that there was a night patrol on the chicken pens.

We went back the next night, but this time we had a plan. We didn't walk down; we crawled down below the weeds. When we got to within sixty or seventy feet of the chicken pens a couple of us started whistling. On came the flashlights, perfect targets. A couple of the fellows who had outflanked us began to throw rocks at them. The beams turned in their direction. Then we threw rocks and scurried to another position. This went on until we heard a loud, clear whistle behind us in the direction of the barracks. Then we got quiet and crept around, staying out of the MPs' way until again they gave up their search for us.

What had happened while the rock throwing was going on was that one of our gang, "Pappy" Starr, had sneaked into the pen with the luscious-looking chickens, snipped the heads off ten of them, and laid the heads out in a neat row. Pappy put some distance between him and the chicken pens before he let us know he had accomplished his mission. We met him near the barracks, picked and cleaned the chickens, buried the feathers and guts in a hole we had dug, and delivered the chickens to the cooks, who cut them up and had them stewing in very short order. Thanksgiving Day we had some rich broth to pour over our rice, and every man got enough chicken to taste. It was a happy Thanksgiving in the Yanks' barracks. Strangely enough, we were never investigated for that caper.

Perhaps the greatest put-down we received from the British was the time Red Cross supplies were distributed in camp. Soon after we arrived at Changi, the SS *Gripsholme* came into port from America. She had been to Canada and the British Isles and America to pick up Red Cross packages for prisoners of war held by the Japanese. She was in Singapore several days to be unloaded. Finally, after many delays and much red tape, her cargo got to the camp at Changi. The British were in charge of distribution. Everyone was getting only a portion of one of the packages because there weren't enough to go around. Then came the day the Yanks were called to come collect their share of the contents of the packages. We wheeled our buggy down to the depot, as the Limeys called it, and made it known that we were there to pick up our ration of Red Cross supplies. The

British put on a couple of cases with a small amount of stuff in them—nothing like the loads we had seen others haul away. The officer who was with us questioned whether we had all that was coming to us. The British officer doing the rationing said that we should consider ourselves lucky that we got anything at all because it was clearly printed on the boxes the stuff came in, **FOR BRITISH AND DOMINION PRISONERS ONLY.** "And America is no dominion of Britain," he added. We certainly couldn't argue with that, but we thought it was awfully short-minded of those responsible for the distribution of the Red Cross packages to take that view.

The British forces in Singapore had some misconceptions of the situation. They could not seem to understand that the Japanese had indeed defeated them on Malay and at Singapore. They operated their forces, whom they did not consider prisoners of war, as though the Japanese forces present were some sort of temporary visitor. For instance: It was insisted on by the powers that were, that is to say the staff of the former Malayan Command, that the British army continue to function as though it were still on active duty and in service to the Queen. Military courtesy was enforced, and there were heavy penalties for the slightest infraction of the regulations, even to the extreme of jail sentences for failure to salute an officer.

A humorous incident happened one day with regard to this rule or regulation. A senior *Houston* officer present was walking down a street, and he was wearing only a pair of green Dutch army shorts, sandals, and a beard. He was smoking his pipe and carrying a walking stick. He had no sort of identification to show that he was a commissioned officer because it had all been lost when the ship was sunk. And, too, the American officers had decided and declared months ago that all military courtesy would go by the board as far as we American servicemen were concerned. As he was enjoying his walk, he was met by two British officers with their pips on the shoulders of their neatly pressed tunics, shoes with gleaming shines, and caps with shiny bills. They appeared to be suitably uniformed to stand a general's inspection. They looked ridiculous really, all decked out in their finest uniforms in the midst of men who were beginning to look like walking skeletons. The officers passed Lieutenant Hamlin and didn't get the expected salute. They stopped and called to the lieutenant. They wanted to know if he had failed to recognize who they were. He said that he didn't think he'd had the pleasure of being introduced to them. They proceeded to inform him that he was in the presence of two lieutenants of the British army (they included their names), and that he had failed to render the hand salute they were entitled to.

When they had finished informing Lieutenant Hamlin as to who they were and what they expected of him, he came to a very stiff attention and said, "Do you recognize who you are speaking to?" The two officers replied that they didn't recognize him. So he continued, "I am Lieutenant Jay Gee H. S. Hamlin, senior officer present and commander in chief of the Asiatic Fleet, United States Navy." As soon as he had finished giving his official title, both British officers assumed a very military attitude, rendering the vibrating hand salute that only the British can do, and said, "We beg your pardon, sir." Then they did a very smart about-face and marched off down the street without further comment. Lieutenant Hamlin chuckled to himself as he resumed his stroll in the sun.

Despite all the troubles with British pomposity and their childlike refusal to recognize and accept the reality that they, too, were indeed prisoners of war, we managed to have some good moments in Singapore. Because the large garrison that had been the Malayan Command, consisting of some 250,000 men, had been captured almost intact, there was an abundance of talent and ingenuity that could create events that did a lot to take everyone's mind off their troubles. These were the people who created some of the best happy hours, or concerts as the British preferred to call them, that I ever saw. At the time we were in Singapore, the Japanese had given permission for these concerts to be held; and as a result, we saw some of the funniest variety shows and some of the best dramas that could be produced. The shows were held once a week and were looked forward to by everybody in the camp, even the Japanese.

We had been in Singapore in Kitchner Barracks only a short while when we were assigned a camp duty, as were all the various units that made up the camp. We Americans were assigned the job of making a vegetable garden that, when completed, was to supply the camp with fresh vegetables. There were some exceptions to the detail, so not all Americans were required to be on the garden detail. We were to supply something like fifty men to the work force of some five or six hundred. The selection of the men to go on this detail was left up to the officers of each unit. In the American unit it was a more or less voluntary project. I volunteered to go on this detail because the work wasn't all that hard, and it gave me a chance to see some of the other parts of the camp and to mix with some of the other people.

The garden was literally carved out of eighteen acres of a rubber plantation. Rubber trees by the hundreds were on the land, and we had to dig them all up and develop seed beds so that the vegetables might grow there. All of the felled trees were collected to provide a supply of firewood for the camp, and most of it was taken to a location from which it was issued at various times. There was one exception. Work crews from the various units were allowed to carry as much of the wood as they could load on their shoulders at the end of each working day. For us it was a windfall. With the fifty men who worked on the project, we usually managed to carry in nearly a cord of wood every day. In fact, the Americans were accumulating such a good supply of firewood that the rules were changed shortly before we left. Each unit was allowed only five tree trunks and whatever branches the other forty men could carry, assuming that it took ten men to carry the five trunks.

12

On January 9, 1943, the American unit then designated as Group 5 left Singapore and Kitchner Barracks. During our stay there, we had developed a very close relationship with a Scottish regiment, The Black Watch; and on the afternoon that we marched out of our barracks, we were piped out by the bagpipes of the Scottish group. We considered it a great honor to be recognized in this way, and every man seemed touched by the thoughts and sentiment behind the honor.

We left the barracks and were loaded in trucks and taken to the railroad station in Singapore. There, in the hot afternoon sun, we sat for some two hours while the citizens of Singapore came to gawk through the pickets of the iron fence which ran around the railroad property. Finally, a train with some ten or twelve boxcars backed into the station and we were put aboard, thirty-five men to a car. The cars were less than half as big as an American boxcar, and thirty-five men made conditions more than crowded. It might have been all right if everyone could have stood up, but we had some with us who were sick enough that they had to lie down. We had left nine of our comrades in the hospital in Selarang Barracks because they were just too sick to travel.

The usual amount of screaming, counting, hollering, and confusion took place as we were loaded into the cars. As soon as the guards and their commander were satisfied that everyone who was supposed to be aboard was aboard, they came down the line and slammed the doors shut. The cars instantly became ovens. It was late in the afternoon, and the hot sun was still heating up the metal sides and tops of the almost airtight boxcars. The only water we had was what we could carry in our one-pint canteens. It wasn't too long before that was exhausted. By then the sun had gone down and it began to get a little cooler. After much juggling and shoving, the men jammed against the door were finally able to get the door open and let in some fresh air, which was badly needed. We shifted positions as we rode along, letting three or four men at a time stand at the door until their sweat-drenched clothes could dry out and they could get a few breaths of clean, fresh air.

About midnight we pulled into a rail yard and the door was closed again. Loud clacks resounded through the frame of the car as the wheels crossed switches, and soon we felt the jerks of the brakes as the engineer brought the train to a halt. In a little while the door was opened, and we were looking out on a passenger platform. We had pulled into the station building at Kuala Lumpur, one of the largest cities on the Malay peninsula. We were told to get out of the boxcars and go to tables that held buckets of rice, stew, and hot tea. The food, no doubt, had been prepared in a Japanese kitchen. It was tasty and did a little to revive us, but the grueling trip had taken a lot out of us.

Since it was so late at night, there were very few civilians present. Indeed, they may have been prevented from coming into the station while our train was there. But who were we to know? We were on the inside looking out. Our stay in Kuala Lumpur lasted for about two hours while the engine was refueled and water put aboard, then we got under way again.

Our next stop was at the town of Ipoh. We got to this station about noon; and again there was a meal of rice, stew, and hot tea waiting for us on the station platform. The food was served by Malay civilians, and though there was little said, it was plain to see that they held little pity for the white captives of the Japanese. There were, however, two "V" signs flashed by a couple of the Malay men who glanced about furtively and held their hands down by their sides. We were allowed to refill our canteens before we were herded back aboard our cars and the train got under way. While we'd been in Ipoh, the American officers had spoken to the guards and arranged for us to keep our box-car doors open. At least there was some flow of fresh air through cars that were beginning to get pretty rank. We had no container to use as a toilet. If a man couldn't get to the door, he just had to relieve himself where he stood.

At first, it was interesting to watch the rubber trees going by as the train rolled along the track. However, after a hundred or so miles, a change of scenery would have been welcomed. The rubber trees just kept going by. A little more than forty-eight hours after we left Singapore, our train pulled into Pria, a little town on the northwest coast of Malaya just south of the Thai border. Rather quickly for the Japanese, we were taken off the train and loaded into small boats on the nearby water. Each boat carried some thirty or forty passengers out to a merchant ship moored in the harbor. The ship was the *Dai Moji Maru*; it was to be our home for the next three days. The transfer of prisoners from the pier to the ship took most of the night, and the first ones loaded on the ship were made to suffer the stifling heat of the holds while the remainder of the transfer operation took place.

Early the next morning the ship got under way with another, larger transport in company. The insignificant convoy was escorted by a small corvette sporting a single three-inch gun on its stern. Traveling in the *Dai Moji Maru* was a repeat of the trip in *Dai Nichi Maru*, except there were no racks to sleep on. Everyone had to find space on the steel deck of the hold. The *Dai Moji Maru* was a smaller ship than *Dai Nichi Maru*, weighing about 3,000 tons, compared to the 5,000 tons of *Dai Nichi*. There wasn't as much space available on the *Dai Moji*, but then there weren't as many passengers either. We received two meals a day consisting of rice with barley in it and a watery stew of some sort of green leafy vegetable, with a cup of hot tea. Time was spent going up the ladder for food, with a rush to the *benjo* if one was lucky, then trying to get back to one's space on the deck in the hold. There was nothing to see topside but the murky brown sea, so the trip was very monotonous for the first two days.

On the third day, at about ten o'clock in the morning, the

hum of aircraft engines was heard. *Dai Moji Maru* blew her whistle and began to pick up speed. Those of us down in the hold could see nothing, but we could hear the bustle as the gun crew on *Dai Moji Maru* manned their weapons and began to track targets. "They're passing overhead," came the shout from the upper deck. *Blam!* went the five-inch AA gun just over our heads. The decks shook and dust filled the hold. For a while we thought we had taken a bomb hit, but word from topside assured us that no bombs had been dropped on that run. Maybe it was just a "reccky" flight (reconnaissance flight). "No! Wait a minute! They're making a turn and coming back. I think this is going to be a firing run. Yeah! I see them falling," reported the unknown voice from topside. Then we heard a sound that was all too familiar—the sound of sand sliding down a tin roof, the sound of bombs falling through the sky above us. The feeling of fear returned, and with it came the realization that we were like sitting ducks on a pond. How could they miss?

Whump!. . . Whump!. . . Whump! They were rather dull sounds, and the somewhat gentle vibration of the ship let us know that we'd been missed that time. "They hit the other ship . . . direct hit . . . it's sinking!" called out our commentator from topside. "Now they've made a turn and are headed back over us . . ." the words were drowned out by the resounding *blam!* from the gun overhead. Then the deathly sound of sliding sand. It was getting louder and louder. Just as it seemed that the sound was going to come into the hold with us, the deck flew up and dust and rust cascaded down from overhead, covering everyone and taking our breath away. I had tried to get a grip on the flat steel deck but could only make a fist as I gathered up empty air. I felt myself lifted off the deck and violently slammed against it as it rose to meet me. Then there was relative quiet.

We had received a near miss forward. Shrapnel had penetrated the side and killed thirty Australians. Another bomb had passed directly through a lifeboat as it was being lowered from the davits, demolishing it and dumping the six or eight Japanese soldiers in it into the sea and then exploding in their midst. Just aft, a bomb had clipped the after gun and exploded, blowing the gun crew over the side and scattering shrapnel across the fantail. In the aftermath of a brush with death, we heard the bombers' motors fade in the distance.

We were told later that the ship that was sunk had been carrying about 500 Japanese civilian workers. None of them survived the sinking. Also on board were a hundred or so Dutch troops. They lost about twenty men. The cargo of the sunken ship consisted of a load of rails, hundreds of picks and shovels, and a couple of locomotives to be used on the railroad—the railroad, we later learned, that we were going to build.

Dai Moji Maru circled the area for more than an hour, picking up survivors from the sunken ship. One incident served to add a touch of humor to an otherwise terrifying experience. One of the Dutch soldiers was pulled aboard with a small orange and white cat sitting on the top of his head. The cat was then and there named "Shipwreck," and it stayed with us at the 100 Kilo Camp until some eight or nine months later when it ran into something bigger one night in the jungle. At sundown the last survivor was picked up, and we continued without further incident.

The next morning before noon, we entered the Salaween River and went to Moulmein, Burma, arriving there just before dark on January 15, 1943. We were sent ashore on barges and were taken immediately to the city prison of Moulmein, some eight or ten blocks from the landing. The prison was a somber-looking red brick building with a twelve-foot wall going completely around it. We entered through an arched gateway and were directed to a group of two-story buildings to our right. At first glimpse, it was easy to see that these buildings had not been used for some time. The wooden floors were covered with a thick coat of dust, and cobwebs hung from the ceilings and walls. The panes in the windows also had their share of dust and grime. Scattered about the rooms were rusted cans of all sizes. Here and there were dried out piles of human feces, and a faint odor of urine filled the air. The grounds surrounding the buildings were knee-high with weeds, with some of the clumps being more than head high. Was this to be our new home? And for how long? We had been told absolutely nothing about the future.

By the time I got into the compound where the buildings were located that we were to be in, the lower floor had been taken. So I struggled up the wooden steps to the balcony of the second floor, not knowing if or when I'd go crashing through the floor, which looked too weak to walk on. Each room looked dirtier than the one before, so I went to the far end and just dropped my gear on the floor of the balcony. That was where I would sleep that night. The next chore was to try to get something to eat. We hadn't eaten since noon or thereabouts, and we were all beginning to feel the effects.

Buddies and groups of three and four scoured all the grounds looking for something to build a fire; however, there was just no wood to be had. Some of the guys had tried to burn the grass, but it was too green to keep a fire going. Finally, there was a shout from near the front of the compound—someone had found the woodpile. There was enough wood there for only a couple of fires; so two were built, and everybody tried to get their cooking done or tea boiled before the coals turned to ashes. Not everyone got something warm that night.

Several of us were still sitting around the heap of warm ashes when suddenly the sound of accordion music filled the compound. We looked up on one of the balconies and saw a Dutch soldier pumping away on an ornate accordion, which sparkled in the weak rays of a nearby oil lamp. The concert lasted for about thirty minutes. Then by ones and twos everybody began to go to their bunks to lie down. The murmur of anxious voices went on all night long as weary and wary souls talked of what might be in store for them in the coming days.

The night air was comfortably cool; however, as the gray light of predawn began to illuminate the eastern sky, the temperature seemed to take a sudden drop and it became uncomfortably cold. From my vantage point on the balcony, I could see several men roaming around the compound, hoping to find any wood that had been overlooked the night before. There was not a stick to be found. But another look through the rooms in our building, which had been hurriedly searched the night before, produced a few chunks of wood and some pieces of broken crates that had been overlooked. These priceless treasures were gathered and a small fire started so that the early risers could have some warmth.

It wasn't too long before the sun came up—a huge red ball floating above the light ground fog, giving our surroundings a different appearance than they had when we arrived. Behind the prison, to the south and not more than half a mile away, was a sight that caused us all to stare in wonder. It was a tall pagoda, perhaps 200 feet high; a very ornate inverted tower with gold leaf covering its entire surface. In the bright sun it gleamed like a cone of fire. Most of us had never seen anything like it before. It was truly an awe-inspiring sight.

Another thing the daylight revealed that had not been noticed the night before was that we had neighbors. From the balcony we could see over the brick wall that was on the east side of our compound, and in the neighboring compound were several dozen Burmese civilian prisoners. They were chained together in groups of five, and they just wandered around rather aimlessly.

We were kept in the red brick prison for five days. Because of nonexistent sanitary facilities, some of our men came down with the first severe cases of dysentery. There would be many more in the following months.

On the sixth day we were herded aboard a train and hauled thirty miles south to Thanbyuzayat, the end of the railroad as it came from Rangoon and now a marshaling yard and transit camp for new workers on the railroad. The camp was later designated as a base hospital camp, and because the Japanese would not put up special markings or allow them to be displayed, the camp underwent several bombing raids in late 1944 when the complexion of the war began to change. Some sixty or more prisoners of war were killed.

As we left the train in Thanbyuzayat, we were required to listen to an absurd talk given by the Japanese commander of the railroad construction battalions. Among other ridiculous statements, he told us we ". . . should weep with gratitude for the Imperial Favors being heaped" upon us. He further stated that the railroad would be built ". . . if we have to build it over the white man's body," and he warned us of the perils of trying to escape. We were to learn that most of the other prisoner groups had been or would be subjected to the same speech as they were brought in to work on the railroad.

Later we were loaded in trucks and taken to 18 Kilo Camp, our first railroad camp.

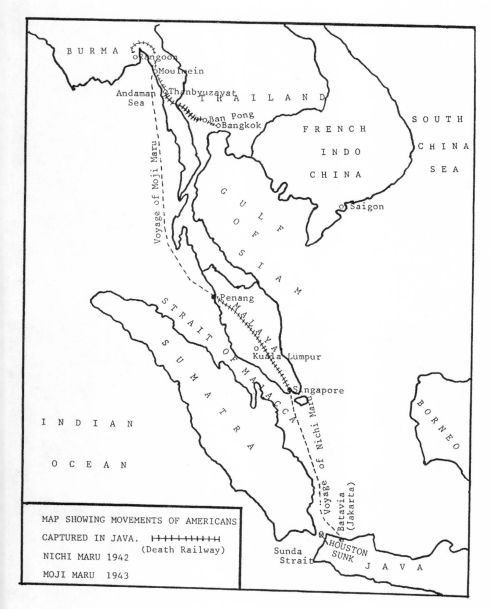

Map depicting movement of prisoners from Java to Burma. (Courtesy of fellow prisoner Ben Dunn)

The last photo of the USS Houston *(CA-30) in Surabaya, Java—late February 1942, a few days before her demise on March 1, 1942.* (Courtesy of USS *Houston* Survivors Association Archives)

The sinking USS Houston *(CA-30) as sketched from memory by Lt. Harold S. Hamlin.* (Courtesy of Kay Hamlin)

Bicycle Camp, Batavia. (Courtesy of USS *Houston* Survivors Association Archives)

Selarang Barracks. (Author's collection)

Artwork by Frank "Foo" Fujita depicting beating of prisoner by Japanese guards. (Courtesy of fellow prisoner Frank "Foo" Fujita)

Prisoners burying their dead. Art by Frank "Foo" Fujita. (Courtesy of Frank "Foo" Fujita)

Prisoners cutting firewood for Japanese train engines. Art by John Wisecup. (Courtesy of John Wisecup)

Prisoners carrying logs back to camp for use as firewood. Art by John Wisecup. (Courtesy of John Wisecup)

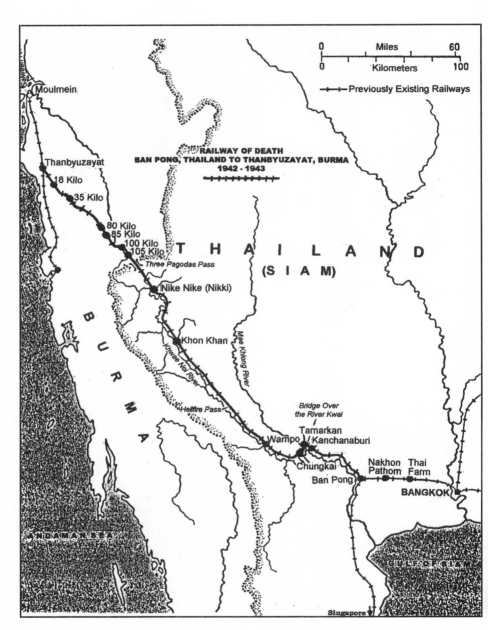

Map of railroad built by allied prisoners between Ban Pong, Thailand (formerly Siam) and Thanbyuzayat, Burma.

Aerial view of American bombing run on the Bridge Over the River Kwai. (Courtesy of USS *Houston* Survivors Association Archives)

Prisoners cheered at the result of American bombs on the Bridge Over the River Kwai. (Author's collection)

Wampo trestle. (Author's collection)

Bridge Over the River Kwai. (Author's collection)

Railroad built by prisoners. (Author's collection)

Thailand-Burma Railway. (Author's collection)

TO ALL ALLIED PRISONERS OF WAR

THE JAPANESE FORCES HAVE SURRENDERED UNCONDITIONALLY AND THE WAR IS OVER

WE will get supplies to you as soon as is humanly possible and will make arrangements to get you out but, owing to the distances involved, it may be some time before we can achieve this.

YOU will help us and yourselves if you act as follows :—

(1) Stay in your camp until you get further orders from us.

(2) Start preparing nominal rolls of personnel giving fullest particulars.

(3) List your most urgent necessities.

(4) If you have been starved or underfed for long periods DO NOT eat large quantities of solid food, fruit or vegetables at first. It is dangerous for you to do so. Small quantities at frequent intervals are much safer and will strengthen you far more quickly. For those who are really ill or very weak, fluids such as broth and soup, making use of the water in which rice and other foods have been boiled, are much the best. Gifts of food from the local population should be cooked. We want to get you back home quickly, safe and sound, and we do not want to risk your chances from diarrhoea, dysentry and cholera at this last stage.

(5) Local authorities and/or Allied officers will take charge of your affairs in a very short time. Be guided by their advice.

Leaflet dropped over Changi POW camp August 28, 1945. (Courtesy of USS *Houston* Survivors Association Archives)

C-47 pilots being briefed for flight to Calcutta, India. (Author's collection)

Liberation Operations—Former prisoners of war waiting to board C-47s at Rat Buri, Thailand, bound for Calcutta, India, on the first leg of journey home. (Author's collection)

Cruiser Houston *survivors returning to the United States after three and a half years in Japanese captivity. Seated left to right: C. L. Thomas, R. L. Yarbro, E. J. Templeman, W. J. Weissinger, V. S. Roberts. Standing: C. A. Back, E. E. Lehnhoff, E. G. Curtin, S. Brown, R. A. Olechno, H. M. Seales. Taken at Bethesda Naval Hospital, Washington, DC.* (Author's collection)

Survivors of the USS Houston *(CA-30) in Washington, DC, September 1945. Front row left to right: Edward J. Templeman, M. M. Marinos, Valdon S. Roberts, Eugene E. Lehnhoff. Back row left to right: Charley L. Thomas, Robert L. Yarbro, and William Weissinger, Jr. Survivors were issued army uniforms at the Calcutta, India, army hospital before departing for U.S. The men on the front row had reported to the navy issue room in Washington for navy blues.* (Author's collection)

WESTERN UNION

DA290 71 GOVT=WASHINGTON DC 14 743P

WILLIAM J WEISSINGER SR=

THE NAVY DEPARTMENT DEEPLY REGRETS TO INFORM YOU THAT YOUR
SON WILLIAM JACOB WEISSINGER JR SEAMAN FIRST CLASS USN IS
MISSING FOLLOWING ACTION IN THE PERFORMANCE OF HIS DUTY AND
IN THE SERVICE OF HIS COUNTRY X THE DEPARTMENT APPRECIATES YOUR
GREAT ANXIETY AND WILL FURNISH YOU FURTHER INFORMATION PROMPT
WHEN RECEIVED X TO PREVENT POSSIBLE AID TO OUR ENEMIES PLEAS
DO NOT DIVULGE THE NAME OF HIS SHIP OR STATION=
REAR ADMIRAL RANDALL JACOBS CHIEF OF THE BUREAU OF
NAVIGATION.

Telegram received from Navy Department by Bill's parents on December 14, 1942.

WESTERN UNION

DA16

51 GOVT=WASHINGTON DC 12 1224A

MR AND MRS WILLIAM J WEISSINGER=
022 12 ST CORPUSCHRISTI TEX=

I AM PLEASED TO INFORM YOU THAT YOUR SON WILLIAM JACOB
WEISSINGER JR SEAMAN FIRST CLASS U S NAVY HAS BEEN SAFELY
RETURNED TO THE UNITED STATES. HIS CONDITION IS GOOD. YOU
MAY EXPECT TO HEAR FROM HIM PERSONALLY AT AN EARLY DATE.
I REJOICE WITH YOU IN THIS GOOD NEWS=
VICE ADMIRAL RANDALL JACOBS THE CHIEF OF NAVAL
PERSONNEL.

THE COMPANY WILL APPRECIATE SUGGESTIONS FROM ITS PATRONS CONCERNING ITS SERVICE

Navy Department telegram received by Bill's parents, September 12, 1945.

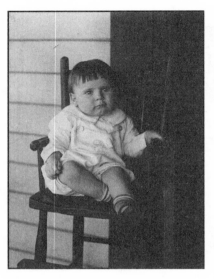

Billy Weissinger, age one, firstborn of Mr. and Mrs. W. J. Weissinger, Sr. Born in Mooreville, Texas, June 13, 1921.

The author as a teenager in San Antonio, Texas.

(Left) On his last visit home before the war started—Billy with his two brothers, Tommy and Robert, in Corpus Christi, Texas. (Above) "Two Billys"—Billy Weissinger, age three (Waco, Texas).

Mr. and Mrs. William J. Weissinger, Jr., February 2, 1946.

Chief Gunners Mate William J. Weissinger, Jr., San Diego, California, summer 1947.

Bill and Eunell with children. Back left Carla (6), back right Linda (8), front left Peggy (2), front right Doug (almost 4). Christmas 1953, Corpus Christi.

Bill and Eunell with family, including at this point seven grandchildren, June 28, 1981, at home of daughter Carla in Maynardville, Tennessee.

Eunell and Bill on their fortieth anniversary, February 2, 1986.

Jewel Daniel—Billy's beloved mother whose faith never wavered that her son would come home again. (She refused to take the navy insurance when he was believed dead.) Picture taken several years before her death the year after Billy's funeral.

13

18 KILO CAMP, BURMA

At first glance, 18 Kilo Camp was a neat-looking place with newly constructed bamboo huts for barracks. The ground was completely barren of grass and trees; there wasn't a piece of vegetation to be seen anywhere on the site, which occupied about three acres. There were two huts, each one about a hundred and sixty feet long by twenty feet wide. They were constructed by using bamboo poles for the frames and covering the roof with *atap* shingles. On the inside was an aisle about six feet wide that ran the length of the hut. On each side of the aisle was a platform raised about two feet from the ground that extended to the outside wall. The platform was covered with bamboo that had been beaten until it split and then was laid out as sort of a mat and tied to the platform frame. Each man was allowed a space about thirty-four inches wide from the aisle to the outside wall, giving him an area measuring roughly three by six feet. This small place on the platform was home.

Earlier, while we had been at Singapore, agreement had been reached between the prisoners and the Japanese that commissioned officers would not be required to do manual labor. So when we got to the railroad camps, the officers were given the assignment of being *kumichos* (squad leaders or group leaders). There were thirty men in a *kumi,* and my *kumicho* was Ens. C. D. Smith, the same officer who had been my division officer aboard ship.

After all the selecting and assigning had been done, the expected work quota was explained to us. Every day each man would be expected to move a cubic meter of dirt (a little more than a cubic yard). That translated into a *kumi* having to move thirty cubic meters per day. We were given picks, chunkles (broad-blade tools similar to a grubbing hoe, but with a wider blade), and shovels and were taken to the work site about two miles from the camp. When we got on the site, it was explained that we were going to build an earthen fill in a low spot in the terrain and that the railroad tracks would be placed on the fill. Bamboo sticks marked the perimeter of the fill, and other bamboo poles showed how high the dirt had to be piled. We were to dig the dirt from a certain area and carry it in burlap sacks. Wires about two and a half feet long would be attached to the front corners of each sack. The sack would then be suspended from the center of a bamboo pole that was long enough to fit on the shoulders of two men. Thus the dirt would be transported.

There were about 2,400 prisoners from 18 Kilo Camp on the work site: approximately 1,000 Dutch, 1,000 Australians, and 400 Americans. The various digging sites were assigned and we were told to go to work. Americans being mostly energetic people, but people who like their leisure time too, usually try to figure out the quickest way to get a job done. The American prisoners of war in 18 Kilo Camp exemplified this rule. Within an hour the American *kumis* had developed a system that would get the most production with the least amount of effort while excavating the dirt, loading the "four-legged wheelbarrows" (or as they were most usually called, the "*yo-yos*"), and carrying the dirt to the nearest dump site. The system was: eight men in the hole, four with picks and four with shovels, and the other twenty-two carrying. Every thirty minutes the men on the shovels would replace the men on the picks, who would replace four men who had been carrying, who would replace the four men on the shovels. This system had the effect of dividing the work so that no single person did all the hard work while others did the easy work. Of course, none of the work was really easy. But the men carrying could take advantage of short periods of rest as the sacks were being loaded. The system worked so well that the Americans reached their quota and got to go back to camp about two o'clock in the afternoon. A *kumi* could return to camp as soon as their quota was finished. The Aussies came in around sundown, and the Dutch came in well after dark. The Dutch complained that such speedy work by the Americans would only increase the quota. The Americans replied in effect: *So what else have we got to do? We're going to be here until the job is finished, let's get it done . . . the Jap's got the gun!* Sure enough, after about a week of early finishes, the quota was raised to one and a half meters per man. The Americans were still able to get into camp before sundown.

When we were released from the work site, the guards would take us to a nearby stream and let us bathe and wash our clothes. Some of the guys began to drink the cool water and fill their water bottles with it. About the third day we had been to the stream, we went into camp and Captain Lumpkin, the army doctor, was on the parade ground. He told the *kumichos* to hold us in formation until he could talk to us. He said, "I've been told that some of you men have been drinking the water in that stream and that you've been filling your water bottles with it. Well, I've got only one thing to say. We don't have anything in this camp to treat cholera with and I don't know anything about cholera. But if sometime you begin to have stomach pains and in a little while you begin to have a high fever and then you go into convulsions for a day or two and then die . . . I can say you probably had cholera." After a few minutes of deathly silence, the *kumichos* said, "FALL OUT!". . . and everyone went back to their huts well aware of a potentially serious situation.

The days were hot, reaching temperatures of 110 to 120 degrees, but the nights, a couple of hours after sunset, were cool. In our digging we had found a lot of sassafras roots, so after supper there would be eight or ten little fires all around the camp on which there were cans of boiling sassafras tea—hot root beer. The tea was very refreshing after we had drunk just plain boiled water all day.

We were paid ten cents a day and got paid every ten days, so on payday we would get a dollar. That wasn't much, but it did allow us to buy an occasional duck egg or two at five cents each; or a caddy of tobacco, about three pounds, for seventy-five cents; or a caddy of *gula mullaca*, palm sugar, for a dollar; a handful of bananas for fifty cents; and, once in a while, mangoes, fifteen cents, and papayas, twenty-five cents.

About a half mile from 18 Kilo was a labor camp containing a number of Burmese. Quite often they would have some kind of celebration with singing and dancing. Since the land was fairly flat between our camp and theirs, we could hear most of the singing and make out a lot of the dancing. Those times served as entertainment on many evenings as we sipped our sassafras tea sweetened with *gula mullaca* and smoked our Burmese tobacco cigarettes.

One night we had a spectacular sight to look at when some of the woodlands about two miles from camp caught fire. It was a real forest fire, with flames shooting up hundreds of feet and showers of sparks flying into the air when some of the huge bamboo stalks exploded. The fire burned nearly all night, but by midnight we'd lost interest in it and went to bed.

At 18 Kilo Camp we worked for the first time with an elephant. There were several large trees that had to be removed from the right-of-way. We cut them down, using the old hand-pulled buck saws, and then dug around the stumps, exposing and cutting all the roots that we could. Finally, when the tree was sufficiently loosened, a *mahout* brought his elephant in and shoved the stump over and carried it off the right-of-way. While the elephant was engaged in this job, he invariably had the urge to defecate. His leavings looked like a large rope and nearly filled the hole we'd dug around the stump. We told our guard that we should get extra pay for having to move all that mess, but he indicated that it was part of the job—so get with it.

As could be expected, all our drinking water now had to be boiled on this work site. At first the Japanese wanted the *kumicho* to do it because he had no other job to do. But we argued with them until it was allowed that a man who was *beoke* (sick) could do the job, since the sick had to work anyway. We used containers the British and Australians called "dixies." A dixie was an oval-shaped pot about eighteen inches long, about eight inches wide, and ten or twelve inches deep. The pots were made of heavy gauge metal and had a metal rod attached the long way so the pot could swivel. Each pot would hold about five gallons. Whenever possible we would have tea to put in the water to give it a little taste. There was nothing as bland as boiled water—sickeningly bland.

14

We stayed in 18 Kilo Camp no more than just a few weeks before we made the first of several moves that would eventually get us into the depths of the Burma jungle. The morning was pleasant as far as the weather was concerned when we started out. We were able to walk to our next camp, the 35 Kilo Camp, which was a distance of only some seventeen kilos. (All camp distances in kilometers were measured from Thanbyuzayat, the railroad depot.) We were still in populated country, and I supposed it was civilized country to a certain extent—but the Japanese nullified that classification to some degree. We moved on foot and had to prepare our own food. There were no rest stops as such along the way. The only rest stop came when a man got so tired that he could not move another step. Then if he was lucky he might persuade the guard to let him wait until a lagging buddy could catch up. Most of the time the answer from the guard would be "*Jalang . . . jalang*," the Malay word for "run." The scenery along the road was beautiful, and we regretted that we couldn't take the time to enjoy it. Burmese who lived along the river which ran beside the road would come out to watch us pass. They showed no sort of emotion as had the Javanese of Java and the Malays of Singapore; they just stood on the side of the road and watched us go by.

Thirty-five Kilo Camp made no great impression because

we were there only a matter of days before we moved to 85 Kilo Camp. We stayed about a week in 85 Kilo and then were moved back down the line to 80 Kilo Camp. The reason? Not known. It seemed to be just the enemy's whim, but there must have been some oriental logic behind it all.

Now we were beginning to get into the jungle proper. The road that ran in front of 80 Kilo Camp had been made recently. "Road" was actually a misnomer, for it was just a set of ox-cart tracks that some of the Burmese conscript labor force had made as they went through the jungle ahead of us by a week or so. Japanese truck drivers had followed the ox-cart tracks between the trees where they could, and that was the "road."

The site of 80 Kilo Camp, had it been under less strenuous circumstances, could have been called beautiful. It was in a grove of teakwood and other trees that we were never able to identify. Less than a quarter of a mile behind the camp was the river, which had a fairly wide bank and was shallow enough for us to bathe. At least it was shallow when we were there, which was in the dry season. The river probably was quite wild during the rainy season; but when we were there, it provided a pleasant scene.

We first started work about five miles north of 80 Kilo and then worked back past the camp to a point about five miles south of the camp. At that point the group known as Group 3 started and worked south about ten miles. At the time, this group was incarcerated in 90 Kilo Camp. We never got to see them because while they were south of 90 Kilo, we were south of 80 Kilo. By the time we got to the place where they had started, they were ten miles south. Nevertheless, we did see the results of their work.

Our biggest project at 80 Kilo Camp was building a bridge. We also built a couple of low culverts, but the bridge was the big job. The reason it was such a big job was because we built the bridge from scratch.

Our first chore was to go up into the hills near the river and cut down tall teak trees that were growing on the steep hillsides. These trees stood from eighty to one hundred feet tall, and they were from two to two and a half feet thick at the butt, or stump. After we cut them down, we had to delimb and debark them, and then carry them on our shoulders down the steep hillsides to the river bank. They were used as pilings and as sleepers on top of the pilings. They had to be carried a distance that varied from one-quarter mile to one-half mile, and it took from eighty to one hundred men to manhandle them down the steep hillsides. After we collected enough for the pilings, piling caps, and sleepers, we wrapped wire around the butt ends so they wouldn't split when they were driven with the two-ton weight that was used as a pile driver. The thin end, which had been the top of the tree, was pointed with an axe, and an iron band was spiked in place to keep the point from splitting as it was pounded into the ground. The timbers used for the piling were about eighty feet long. The pilings were driven by hand.

To drive the pilings, a tower was constructed of saplings about six inches in diameter at the butt end. The saplings were wired together to form the legs and braces of the four-sided structure which was shaped much like a windmill tower. The tower was forty feet tall and on the very top was an arrangement of pulleys—one each on opposite sides of the tower—with a thick rope run through them. On one end of the rope was a 2,400-pound weight. The weight was about three feet tall, one foot in diameter on the top end and eighteen inches in diameter on the bottom, and it had a hole through the center going from top to bottom. The hole in the weight fit around a pipe that acted as a guide when the weight was pulled to the top of the tower and then released to slide down the pipe and land on top of the piling. It took eighty men, forty on each side, to lift the weight. In order that everyone would pull at the same time, a guard sat atop the tower and called cadence. He would call out, "*Ichi, ni, ya san, YON!*" (One, two, and three, four.) On *ichi* everyone would pull with one hand; on *ni* the other hand would be used to pull the hand line; on *san* another pull with the first hand; and on *YON!* everyone would let go of the rope. The weight would then fall the forty feet it had been hoisted and the process would begin all over again. It took 200-300 strokes to drive the piling deep enough to satisfy the Japanese. That number of strokes times the forty-four pilings that were driven resulted in a lot of *ichi, ni, ya san, YONs* being called out before the job was finished. The pulling of the weight was in addition to carrying the eighty-foot timber into the river and standing it up, then setting the pipe into a hole that had been drilled in the top of the piling.

We had been in 80 Kilo Camp only a week or so when some of our men began to become so sick they couldn't stand up. It was then that our captors converted one of the huts into a hospital; but that, too, was a misnomer because the doctors, Doctor Lumpkin of the army and Doctor Epstein of the navy, were given no medical supplies to speak of. They were issued a couple of small bottles of quinine, and that was it.

The first man we lost in the jungle was F. Kondzela, U.S. Navy, seaman first class. He died of malaria. It was a stunning blow when we came into camp one afternoon and were told that he had died only a couple of hours earlier. He died March 13, 1943. That night J. H. White, U.S. Navy, died of malaria. These were the first deaths in the jungle, and they made us realize just how vulnerable we were and how helpless. But things got worse.

While we were working at cutting the trees off the hillsides and preparing them for pilings and caps and sleepers, our work hours were from five in the morning to about six-thirty in the afternoon. Our noon meal was carried to the job site by the cooks and served there. The dry season was beginning to reach its hottest period, the usual temperature being around 125 degrees in the middle of the afternoon and then cooling off to the 100-degree mark by the time we went back to camp. And since the work site was between hills, there was very seldom any breeze to be felt. We were working under these conditions on a diet that consisted of a pint of boiled rice covered with a thin vegetable stew for breakfast, the same thing for noon, and we had it again when we finished the day's work. Because we lacked the facilities to wash the rice thoroughly, it was always contaminated with weevils and worms. Our noon meal would be a little cleaner—if we had time to sort out all the bugs, which we didn't always have.

After we had finally gotten all the necessary timbers onto the job site, the work hours changed. We went on an eighteen- to twenty-hour shift. We left camp at the same time in the morning that we always had, but we didn't get back to our beds until one-thirty or two o'clock the next morning. Then after a couple of hours in camp (during which time we hardly rested), we were herded out to the job again for another twenty-hour go. This schedule was held for two months—April and May 1943.

The weather was extremely hot and dry. The trail that was used as a road soon became a river of dust six inches deep. It was so hot by noon that the cooks who carried our food to us had to wrap rags around their feet and legs to keep from coming in direct contact with the dirt, which was so hot it would cause blisters to form. The dust was finer than talc; and as we marched through it, it would rise in stifling clouds, stopping up our nostrils and making it difficult to breathe.

The usual routine while we were on the long hours was that work would go on as usual until about four-thirty in the afternoon. At that time the guards would cut a few men loose from the regular tasks and have them go out in the jungle and gather bamboo. They would stack all the bamboo on four corners of the site, piling it up to heights of some eighteen or twenty feet. Then when it got too dark to see what we were doing, piles of bamboo would be lit off. That was our light until the pile burned down, which was usually at one-thirty or two o'clock in the morning. So although we didn't have the hot sun to contend with after dark, we did have another source of almost unbearable heat, for bamboo burned terribly hot. There was just no relief from the heat or the dust . . . or the hunger.

The first few days of the extended working hours, we were given a bonus as we left the camp in the morning. Sometimes it was a boiled egg or a piece of *gula mullaca*. One time it was a pack of ten Japanese cigarettes. But this practice lasted only about a week, and again we were just herded out like cattle.

Of course, the long hours and hard conditions began to take a toll on the men able to work, and the work force started to become smaller; but that was no problem for the Japanese. They just went through the hospital and got anyone they thought looked healthy enough to stand up—men who had been on reduced rations for days. Rations for the sick were one-half those given to the working men. Usual Japanese logic.

We were fortunate that no one suffered a bodily injury. We only had to contend with dysentery, malaria, dengue fever, and malnutrition—at first. It is a true wonder that no one was bitten by a snake, for there were many there, and we had to go around barefooted and wearing G-strings. Some of the luckier men had hats to ward off the hot sun. I had one but soon discovered that a hat was not that much of an asset. After dark the gnats would swarm under its brim and bite my eyelids, my ears, and the folds in the skin of my neck until the blood ran. There were not many happy times in 80 Kilo Camp.

We did have a couple of exciting moments. The first one occurred when one of the Japanese engineers found a tiger's den while he was rambling around in the jungle near the work site. When he found the den the mother tiger was gone, but there were two little cubs in it. So he picked them up and brought them into camp. He worked hard building the cubs a cage and was happy to have a couple of pets there in the jungle. He had them about three or four days when one night, just as everyone had settled down, there was a blood-curdling scream from the vicinity of the engineers' hut. Everyone cringed in their beds and tried to imagine what had produced such a scream. The tiger cubs had been forgotten for the moment. Then another scream and the crash of breaking wood. Like a flash we realized what it was. It was the mother tiger, and she had found her cubs. Lights began to show in the Japanese hut, but the crashing continued for a few more minutes. Then all was quiet. The next morning we saw that the cage had been reduced to a few pieces of wood that were hardly good enough for kindling.

The next bit of excitement came about when one of the Japanese engineers committed suicide after he had been reprimanded by his sergeant. The reprimand had taken place on the job site, and we prisoners hadn't given it much thought because it was a common occurrence. Some officer was always slugging some noncom, and some noncom was always slugging some poor private, so to us it was just another example of Japanese military "courtesy." That night when all the camp was relatively quiet and everyone was trying to ignore the mosquitoes and get some sleep, the roar of an explosion burst through the camp. We held our breath and tried to imagine what had happened and wondered if there would be another explosion. All was silent, but over in the Japanese hut lights began to glow. And though we couldn't hear plainly what was being said, we did sense some excitement over there. The next morning we learned that the reprimanded, embarrassed engineer had gone into the jungle a few hundred yards behind the camp and placed the muzzle of his rifle in his mouth, pulled the trigger with his big toe, and had blown off the top of his head. He was cremated on a huge pyre the other engineers built and burned, and his ashes were presumably sent back to Japan to receive a hero's welcome. We wished more of the Japanese would become embarrassed.

In the last days of May 1943, we finally completed the work at 80 Kilo Camp. We had built the bridge and its approaches, and everything was in readiness to receive the tracks as soon as crews could begin laying them. As we finished the work at this camp, the monsoon days were just beginning. The monsoon season runs from May until November, and all the land that has been turned into dust during the dry season becomes a sea of mud. Hollows between hills become streams, streams become rivers, and rivers become raging torrents as the land attempts to divest itself of the continually falling rain. The only things that are not moved by the running water in the south Burma jungle during the rainy season are the granite mountains that stick up above the plains like the spine of a dinosaur. There is not a dry spot to be found anywhere.

We had an early breakfast the morning we left 80 Kilo Camp because the cooks, with the help of six or seven other men, had to dismantle the kitchen and get the cooking pots moved and set up again at 100 Kilo Camp—our next destination. They would have food ready for us at the new camp when we arrived there sometime in the late afternoon, barring any problems. The cooks and their kitchen went by truck. We followed an hour or so later on foot.

15

100 KILO CAMP, THROUGH THE BURMA JUNGLE

When we started out for 100 Kilo Camp, the sky was filled with scattered clouds. We'd been having afternoon showers for about a week, and they were welcomed because they cooled things off some and gave us a chance to have a cold bath. The road here past 80 Kilo was even worse than the one we had traveled on from 30 Kilo Camp. Really there was no road, for trucks had not been driven between the trees enough to establish any definable tracks. All we could do was go in the direction the guards pointed out to us.

Humidity was heavy all morning. By noon it had turned to rain, a kind of slow drizzle that gradually soaked through all our packs and kit bags. No matter about getting our clothes wet—we had none. Most everyone wore only a G-string and was barefooted. The few who did have trousers and shirts and boots were miserable, given the circumstances.

As the black of night enveloped the jungle, it began to rain harder—drops now fell in a veritable torrent. There was no wind, so the effect was that of walking through a lake. I firmly believed that if a person had turned his face upward and breathed, he would have drowned right there—standing up.

It was impossible to see more than a few inches away; and one had to be alert to a called warning of slippery roots or a washed-out ditch in the path or a low-hanging limb that could break a neck. There was a continuous stream of cursing, swearing, and cries of pain as an unwary man stepped into an unseen ditch, sending his pack sprawling along the wet jungle floor. Or when another would stub his bare toes on a root, or worse yet, a piece of granite sticking up in the path. He couldn't take the time to see if the toe had been severed from his foot; he could only hope that it hadn't been and that he wouldn't bleed to death before he got to camp. At other times a man might run, or more likely slip, into a low-hanging limb that would strike his Adam's apple with such force that he was rendered speechless for more than a few minutes. Or the limb might rake along the side of his head and take off a patch of skin as wide as his hand. Soon he would begin to taste the blood as it mixed with the rainwater and ran into his mouth.

For many, this struggle went on all night. For me, it lasted about five hours. I staggered into camp about eleven o'clock that night. Some didn't get in until well after daylight. But getting into camp was no real relief. We had been moved to a camp that had formerly been occupied by some of the conscript labor force: Indians, Malays, and Burmese who had been drafted by the Japanese to work on the railroad. And they had left the huts in shambles. A few oil lamps were burning in the hut I was assigned to; and by their flickering light, I could see the water-covered bamboo platform that was supposed to be our bed. The aisle through the center of the hut had turned into a river when the heavy rains began, and it would remain so for the next five months, June through October.

Because of the heavy rains, the cooks had not been able to set up the kitchen; and so there was no food, warm or otherwise—only a can of hot tea, if one wanted to struggle through 200 feet of black jungle guided by the glimmering fires in the kitchen. I turned down the offer and waded up the aisle until I found a space that no one was claiming, threw my awkward, cumbersome pile of gear against the outside wall, and climbed up on the platform and stretched out—face up, under a stream of water pouring in through a leak in the roof. I flopped over and just lay there wondering what I had ever done to be the subject of such a tortured life. After a few minutes I raised up and began to examine myself to see what damage I had suffered.

Fortunately, it was nothing more than a few scratches on my face, neck, body, legs, and feet. No broken bones, no missing digits or eyes.

I managed to stay awake for about an hour but finally had to go to sleep; I was about to drop in my tracks. The sleep was not restful because all night long men kept straggling into camp. As they arrived and were led into the hut, some friend or shipmate would be happy that another of his buddies had managed to make it and they would talk for a while. Also, the roof leaked and it seemed that just when I'd get situated where one stream would miss me, another one would start and I would have to rearrange my position. All the talk and dodging the leaks had one good aspect to it—it kept my mind off the gnawing hunger pangs in my stomach.

Daylight finally arrived and the Japanese were not going to make us work that day. It was, they said, a *yasemae* day, a day of rest. But really it wasn't because we stayed busy trying to mend the roof and arranging our sleeping spaces so they would be more comfortable. Also, we tried to get all our belongings dried out. It was a very busy rest day.

The second day we were in 100 Kilo Camp was a work day. We were taken to the right-of-way just behind the camp. Our first job was to remove several clumps of bamboo that were growing there. Bamboo has to be nature's most obstinate plant when it comes to removing it from the earth. It has millions of tiny roots, every one as strong as a steel cable. The clump has to be totally dug up; there is no such thing as just digging around it and pulling it out of the ground.

While several of my *kumi* were busy trying to get the bamboo clumps dug up, I and three or four of my shipmates were assigned to help one of the engineers lay out the lines for the fill that was going to have to be put in at this place. He had an engineer's level and transit set up and then instructed us on how to hold the rod, the measuring stick used by construction engineers, and where to stand, and so forth. We spent most of the day moving the rod around and driving stakes wherever the engineer told us to. It looked like it might be a fairly easy job, here at 100 Kilo Camp.

The heavy rain of the night we moved in was not repeated

for almost a week. We would have showers nearly every day, but nothing as heavy as it had been that night. As the days moved on, however, the showers began to last longer and longer each day.

In the meantime, we had started building the fill. It was to be the largest fill we would ever have to build. It was nearly a quarter of a mile long and measured about twenty feet at its highest point. The roadbed where the track would lay was to be about ten feet wide and the sides of the fill were to slope at sixty degrees, so that meant the base had to be over a hundred feet wide. The first few days it looked mighty pitiful, with just a few piles of dirt scattered out through the grass that then covered the right-of-way; but these few pitiful piles of dirt represented some ten or more hours of labor each by 300-400 men. We had built the fill up to a height of about six feet when the rains began in earnest. The guards continued to take us out to the job until it became obvious, even to them, that as we tried to stack the mud up, we were pulling down more than we could stack. This was around the first of July.

It had rained heavily for three or four days and had flooded and washed out what road there was so that no trucks could get to 100 Kilo Camp with supplies of rice and vegetables. So within the week we had to go on reduced rations. The food situation at one point got so bad that for the noon meal, which was brought out to the job site, one man's ration would be six tablespoons of boiled rice, half a whitebait (a small fish about the size of a minnow), and seven or eight peanuts. The morning and evening meals were not a lot better. Meat of any kind was nonexistent.

When finally the Japanese were convinced that no progress could be made on the earthen fill during the heavy rains, they switched the men of the 100 Kilo Camp to making ballast for the railroad. We first went to the mountains to make ballast on the Fourth of July. As we were going down the road, someone mentioned the date; and we all fell silent for a moment—remembering the Fourth of July just a year ago.

In the new job we were taken up in the mountains, given twelve- and fifteen-pound sledgehammers, and made to break the large granite boulders into fist-sized rocks that would be used for ballast along the 250 miles of railway. Some of the

Japanese engineers acted as powder monkeys; that is, they would set the charges of dynamite in holes that had been drilled by prisoners and blast out huge chunks of the granite. Due purely to luck, no prisoner of war was ever killed by the blasting operations, but several engineers lost their lives. I remember one incident in particular.

One crew of about thirty prisoners had been taken into the mountains where they drilled some forty or fifty holes ten feet deep or so. Then the holes were packed with dynamite charges, the caps and fuses were put in place, and everyone was taken out of the area. The blast area was near a road, so the Japanese stopped traffic until the blast could be made. They lit the fuse and waited the amount of time that was supposed to elapse before the blast went off. Nothing happened. They waited another thirty minutes or so. Still no blast. So three of the engineers decided that they would go up and see why the dynamite had failed to go off. They were shouting back to those who stayed behind what they were doing and where they were, when all of a sudden the blast went off and pieces of rock mangled the three engineers. I was in the bed of one of the trucks that had been stopped directly in front of the blast; but as the engineers had started to go into the area where the dynamite had been placed, all of us American prisoners got out and hunkered down on the lee side. After the blast, we found chunks of granite as large as a man's head lying in the bed of the truck, and one of the seats had been smashed.

All work was stopped that day, but early the next morning prisoners were put to work building a huge pyre of bamboo. The following day the pieces and scraps of the engineers that had been found in the blast area were piled on the bamboo and cremated. When the ashes had cooled, a handful was put in each of three boxes and sent off, presumably to Japan.

Two Americans had died in 100 Kilo Camp in June. A. J. Lindsley, USN, died of dysentery on June 1, 1943, and C. W. Benner, USN, died June 26, 1943, also of dysentery. In all probability, at least an equal number of Dutch and Australian troops died during that time. But the rainy season and all its attending problems had not really afflicted us yet.

July and August were the deadly months, for it was then

that all the problems of malnutrition compounded the devastation of malaria and the two prevalent types of dysentery. Literal starvation was the principal cause of the malnutrition. Food supplies became so low during several periods that foraging parties were sent into the jungle to find edible plants and roots and to look for stray oxen that had become useless to their owners because of split and diseased hooves and had been released in the jungle to make their own way. During this time the Dutch, on more than one occasion, had dog carcasses hanging up in their kitchen. Even the Japanese organized hunting parties and went into the jungle to hunt wild boar.

On one of the trips into the jungle to look for oxen, the American hunters found one; however, it was so poor and lean that it produced only enough meat for each of the some 350 Americans to get six or eight three-quarter-inch cubes in their stew one night. The men said that the hide weighed more than the meat that came from it.

I had worked in the rock-breaking crew no more than a week when one night, just as all the work crews got into camp, someone asked me if I hadn't been an auto mechanic before I got into the service. I said that I had fooled around with cars and knew a little about them. My questioner said, "Well, they're looking for a couple of guys to go to a Jap motor pool just up the road. Why don't you go?" I found out that one of the officers was handling the assignment and went to him and told him that I would like to have the job. He told me that I had it and that instead of going out with the regular work detail the next morning, I and two army men would be picked up and taken to the shop in a truck.

The next morning, after the hullabaloo of getting the work details out of camp, a truck pulled in and the three of us got aboard and were taken about three miles to the motor pool shop. The shop was manned by three privates, a sergeant, and a lieutenant. There was a small three-bay repair shop, a hut for the Japanese crew, and a small cookhouse in the camp. Only the lieutenant could come close to speaking and understanding English. My first job was to repair a flat on a utility truck about the size of a pickup. It was a British Leyland, and the front wheels were two discs bolted together around the hub with an-

other ring of bolts just inside the rim. The Japanese sergeant
asked me if I knew how to get the tire off, and I told him I did.
I took all the bolts out of the hub and then began to remove the
ones just below the rim. Instead of loosening them and letting
the tire expand a little at a time, I took each bolt out as I loosened it. When I got to the last two bolts, the two discs flew apart
and knocked me down. One disc went one way and the other
disc another way, causing a heck of a commotion. The sergeant
came running over to me and kicked me a couple of times,
screaming, "*Bakaro! Bakarodaro!*" and some other gibberish. It
was easy to see that he was unhappy with the way I had done my
first job. He finally cooled off and left me to finish putting the
patch on the tube and putting the tire back on the rim, but he
never liked me much after that.

The first three days we acted more as mechanic's helpers
than anything else. On the fourth day we were given a definite
task. As a result of all the rain, the road by the shop had become
almost a river of its own, and water threatened to run into the
shop. So the sergeant decided a floor was needed. He told us
that we were to go across a stream behind the shop and cut some
of the trees there for logs. The logs would then be laid on the
ground inside the shop to raise the elevation of the floor above
the road.

In the dry season the stream behind the shop was probably
no more than a narrow brook, but in the rainy season it had become a fairly deep and fast running stream about thirty feet
wide, making it hard to cross. We managed to get across and
tied a rope to a tree on each side of the stream. Thus we had a
hand hold as we went back and forth to get the logs and carry
them back to the shop. It took us a couple of days to cut enough
trees to provide the number of logs that we would need. Each
log was cut two meters long so that two men could carry it. It
took us another day to get them across the stream and then we
were ready to begin laying them down on the floor.

We had carried in enough logs to make one row from the
back of the shop to the front and were beginning the second
row. I was on the end that would butt against the first row, and
standing on that row with his toes hanging over the end of the
log in place was the sergeant. He was standing there making all

sorts of noise and indicating that they wanted the logs to be placed as closely together as possible. I tried to tell him to move his feet back so the log I was holding wouldn't clip his toes when I dropped it in place, but he was too busy being boss to hear. The log was very heavy and I had to let it go. When I did, it caught his big toe. He let out a scream and in a flash had given me several sharp blows on each shoulder, using a *mahout* stick he was carrying. I thought my neck was broken because my arms were paralyzed for nearly an hour after the flogging. Eventually the feeling did come back, but the bruises and pain remained for about a week afterward.

While we had been cutting the logs for the shop floor, I had stepped across a clump of bamboo that we had to cut out of our way. In the process a small sliver of bamboo had punctured the skin just behind my left ankle. I didn't pay much attention to it; but in a couple of days it began to ache, and I could see that it was beginning to fester. I treated the small sore in the usual way that I treated other such scratches, by packing salt around it overnight and then pouring hot water over it in the morning and again at night when I got back to camp. It didn't respond to the treatment at all. The festered area began to get larger, and that frightened me because I knew it was the beginning of a dreaded tropical ulcer. Our experience had been that once this disease of the skin started, there was no way to stop it. It just continued to fester, destroying all living flesh as it grew until it had consumed the major portion of a leg or arm or whatever part of the body it was on. Mine had grown to the size of a dime and was very painful, but I continued to work on it. There was no way to keep a bandage on it—even if I'd had one. So I waded around shin-deep in the jungle mud all day and would pack salt around the sore at night and pour hot water on it in the mornings.

In the meantime, I nicked my left shin on another piece of bamboo, and within a week it had festered to the size of a quarter. My leg became inflamed, and it began to look like I was a prime candidate for blood poisoning. A few more days and I couldn't stand to put my weight on my left leg; I had to quit work.

The prognosis was not good. We all knew that when a man

became immobile, he was on his way to the grave. A man had to keep going. He had to stay on his feet; otherwise he was dead. We were seeing examples of it every day. My only hope was to keep eating. The popular slogan all through our POW experience was: "Your ticket home is in the bottom of your mess kit."

I went on the sick list and was allowed to stay in my bunk. A few days after I had been on the sick list, I had my first attack of malaria; with its symptoms of chills and fever. Fortunately, we had a meager supply of quinine at that time. The dose given to each patient was not enough to effect a cure, but it did serve to lessen the debilitating effect for a while. I had terrific chills all day one day. At times I thought I would freeze to death; I shivered and shook and there was no way to control it. Blankets and shelter halves were piled on me, but I was still cold and shaking. Finally, just after dark the chills left and I began to have fever. That night I went into a fitful sleep and had nightmares all night long; my head felt as though it would split into pieces at any moment. I found that if I would moan in a certain key it seemed to relieve the pain in my head. So I moaned. The fellow on my right would slam his fist across my chest every once in a while to make me stop because I was disturbing his sleep. But after waiting a minute or two I would begin to moan again.

The cycle of chills and fever lasted three or four days; I couldn't remember. All the days and nights seemed to run together and I lost track of time. Then one morning I woke up feeling fairly good. I was terribly weak, but I had no chills and no fever. And I managed to eat a few bites of the boiled rice and the thin weed stew that had been served for breakfast that morning—my first food in several days. I had been able to get down some hot tea during the days that I had the chills and fever, but no kind of solid food. The mixture they had served for breakfast would have gagged a maggot, but I did manage several spoonfuls. Then I looked at my leg because I became conscious of a feeling of fever in it. The ulcer on my ankle had grown to the size of a quarter and the one on my shin was as big as a silver dollar. Both were as black as a lump of coal; they were on their way to consuming my left leg.

In a day or two I could see a tiny speck of white in the center of the ulcer on my shin; it was my shinbone showing through.

A couple of days later, the tiny white speck had grown to the size of a dime and looked like a tiny spotlight surrounded with darkness. I lay on my back and began to think of home, my mother and sisters and brothers, and my daddy. I began to recall the good times I had as a child in Texas and wondered if I would ever see that kind of life again. At the moment it looked very doubtful that I would. I was not alone in this suffering. All through the hut lay men who were in the same condition—most of them actually in worse shape, for I was one of the less sick. At least I could eat.

It was about this time that Doctor Epstein came into our hut to hold sick call and announced that the Japanese had just delivered medical supplies to 100 Kilo Camp: a five-gallon can of Epsom salts and about two pounds of iodaform, an antiseptic used by veterinarians to treat cuts on livestock. Those who were conscious enough to understand what he had said got a laugh out of that. Eighty percent or more of the men in camp had dysentery in varying degrees; Epsom salts was the last thing that was needed in our camp. But again that was Japanese logic.

Since there was no treatment for tropical ulcers, I continued to use the only thing available—hot water. Eight men had been allowed by the Japanese to stay in the hut and care for the sick. There wasn't a lot they could do medically, but they were able to help the weak guys to the latrine, bring them food or drink if they were able to eat, and hold their head or their hand as they died. The men had all volunteered for this job. They were on duty twenty-four hours a day every day. They kept a fifty-five-gallon drum of water boiling around the clock and would bring a man as much as he desired any time he called for it. So I set a schedule for myself. I poured hot water over my ulcers every four hours night and day. I would call out at any hour, and the orderlies would bring me a number two can, a little more than a pint, of the boiling water. Within a week I could pour the water over the ulcer while it was still boiling in the can. I poured hot water for nearly two weeks, each time looking closely to see if I could detect any change in the appearance of the two awful sores on my leg.

After the first three or four days, it became apparent that the sores had stopped enlarging; however, they remained as black as coal. The orderlies would bring my morning can of water just at dawn so that they could serve breakfast to the guys who could eat while the food was still fairly warm. One morning, after about two weeks of pouring the boiling water on my leg, I noticed in the weak light of the dawn a thin line of pink flesh outlining the ulcer on my shin. It was no wider than a human hair, but it was there and it was pink. Healing had started. A few days later the ulcer at my ankle showed the same encouraging sign. It had taken more than a month, but finally I had the black portion on my shin down to the size of a quarter and the one on my ankle to the size of a dime. Nevertheless, the pink covering was proud flesh and would not develop into skin. The area remained puffy-looking and drained a clear fluid continuously, but it wasn't black and it wasn't taking my leg.

During the month that the ulcers had stayed black, I had another round of malaria and also had a touch of dysentery. The small dose of quinine had helped with the malaria, and I was given rice that had been burned into charcoal to control the dysentery. I didn't know if it actually worked or not, but something kept the dysentery from becoming acute and killing me as it had killed and continued to kill my shipmates.

Although we lost only two men shortly after we had moved into 100 Kilo Camp in June, many at that time were very sick and the July death loss increased to four. At the same time, the Dutch and Australians were suffering the same losses. In fact, the Dutch probably suffered even heavier losses, for it seemed that when one of them became bedridden he gave up and died within a few days. (The Dutch troops referred to were the Javanese and Eurasians who made up most of the Dutch army in Java, though there were a large number of white Dutch there as well.) A cemetery had been established across the railroad right-of-way behind the camp, and men were kept busy digging graves. There would be three to four funerals every day, it seemed. In the morning we would hear the American taps echoing through the jungle as an American was put in his grave. Shortly afterward, the sound of the Australian "Last Post" would be heard, and then a bugle would sound as the Dutch laid their dead in the ground.

There were no caskets. The bodies would be wrapped in

rice sacks made of rice straw; a fiber rope was tied around the bundle; and the body was put in the shallow grave, usually only two or three feet deep. Each grave was marked by a cross made by men of each nationality. And before we left 100 Kilo Camp, an entrance to the cemetery was erected featuring a handcarved panel above the gate that read, "**ALLIED POW CEMETERY * ANGANAN 100KM CAMP.**" There was also a hand-carved cross that stood eight feet tall and was inscribed on the vertical member, **IN MEMORY OF**, and on the horizontal arm, **AUS-TRALIAN-DUTCH-BRITISH-AMERICAN 3 & 5 BRANCH PRISONERS OF WAR.** The message continued on the vertical member . . . **WHO DIED IN BURMA**. There were more than 200 graves in that cemetery.

The critical month was August 1943. That month fifteen Americans died in 100 Kilo Camp—one every two days. It got so bad that when one went to sleep at night, he wondered if he would wake up in the morning. On more than one occasion, a man would wake up and find that the man he had talked to the night before had died during the night. The death rate was a serious concern for more than one reason. The number one concern was, of course, when would this senseless dying stop? The other concern was that there were only so many lives in camp. If the dying continued, all the numbers would be used up and each of us would have to face our turn. It seemed that the only end was for everyone to die.

The Japanese continued to turn deaf ears to pleas for mercy and requests for medical supplies—or even decent food. The situation got so bad that for a two-week period that August, the Japanese commandant at 100 Kilo put out an order that no one was allowed to die on Wednesday because too much time was being lost by men digging graves and burying the dead. This order resulted in an accumulation of bodies which would decompose very rapidly in the jungle heat. When the stench of the decomposing bodies reached the commandant's hut, he rescinded his order and allowed men to die and be buried every day of the week.

The month of August was also my critical month, for it was near the end of that month that my ulcers began to show some signs of improvement. During that time I lay in different areas of the hut and watched many of my shipmates, most of whom had become closer than a brother, waste away and die. Some remained conscious to very near the end—conscious enough to realize that they were dying and that there wasn't a thing anyone could do to prevent it. Others, in the depths of coma-like sleep, died more easily.

It was during this time, when death was a daily occurrence, that I saw a phenomenon that I would never forget. It was guys within hours of death, but conscious, who would see and speak to guys who had died in the previous few days. They would be lying down quietly with two or three buddies around, nobody speaking, when suddenly the deathly ill man would begin to have a conversation with someone who had died within the last week. When this first began to happen, those standing around the sick man would tell him that the person he was speaking to had died two, maybe three, days ago. The dying man would respond that he didn't believe them because he could see this person standing before him with them. The conversations would last from just a few minutes to up to thirty minutes or so. This unusual occurrence didn't happen every time a man died, but it did take place often enough that it remained a nagging memory for me on many occasions and caused me to wonder what does happen after the thing we call death occurs.

By the middle of September, I had gained enough strength back to attempt to walk again. After lying on one's back for nearly two months, one loses the ability to walk. He doesn't even know how. He has to learn all over again. It was nearly a month before I could walk without assistance. The first week I had to have someone hold me up; I couldn't bear my weight on my legs. The second week I was able to get about with a cane but needed someone to help me get up and sit down, or turn. I was able to operate my legs and could bear the weight, but I could only go in a straight line. After two weeks I could do pretty well with the cane, and I finally got enough strength to do away with that aid. By now it was late October 1943.

The month of October was the deadline the Japanese had set for completing the railroad. In June and July the rains had caused a slowdown, but as the rains began to slacken in August and September, the Japanese began their "*speedo*" program. Again, for those still able to work, it was twenty-four-hour days.

The enemy was going to have trains running over the railroad if it killed every man who worked on it.

One day near the end of September, we heard the roaring sound of a diesel engine. It was the track-laying crew approaching 100 Kilo Camp. Just to the north of the camp was a slight grade, and the diesels had to put on full power to go up it. The system being used was as follows: The railroad ties would be carried ahead far enough so that a couple of lengths of rail could be laid on them, then the rails would be fed off the truck and tacked down. When all its ties and rails had been unloaded, the truck would return to the supply yard and pick up a new load while another truck was delivering ties and rails. It took this detail only a day to get out of hearing distance of 100 Kilo Camp. The spiking crews followed, then came the ballast crews. By the second week in October, steam trains were using the railroad. And although the railway was not completely finished, a big celebration was held in Nike Nike (Nikki), Thailand, on October 20, when the north end met the south end and the final spikes were driven. One month later, November 20 and 21 were set aside as days of celebration and jubilee by the Japanese, marking the day the railroad was completed.

By November the rains had slackened to a considerable degree, there being more sunny days than rainy ones; and the exhausted and spent prisoners began to regain some of their spirit. Work had eased a good bit, and men spent the occasional *yasemae* days putting all their clothing and bedding in the sun to rid them of lice and bedbugs which had plagued them through the wet months. The food did not improve, so the beriberi, pellagra, and other forms of malnutrition remained.

Most of the work now consisted of maintenance along the line, and the Japanese didn't seem to be in the hurry that had been so all-consuming during the building of the railroad. It was soon announced that by the last of December we would be taken south to Thailand to a rest camp. We were still in 100 Kilo on Christmas Day 1943, and it was beginning to look like the assurance of the rest camp was just another empty promise of our captors.

Christmas Day 1943 was one of the saddest days of my life. For a week before, nearly every man who was able began to work on something he could give to a buddy on Christmas Day. C. E. Carroll and I got with Charley Green, who had gone into the bakery business, and had him bake a cake for us to give to one of our buddies, E. A. Hatlen. Hatlen had beriberi, and for a while it looked as though he was going to recover from it. But suddenly, seemingly overnight, he took a turn for the worse. We had the cake baked and took it to him in his bed. At this time he was so swollen, from head to foot, that he was nearly twice his normal size. He could barely open his eyes enough to see the cake, but he did look at it. Then he said, "I can see it but I can't eat a bite of it . . . thanks." Tears welled up in our eyes and we got terrible lumps in our throats. Hatlen lay down, and we could see that he had splits in the skin of his back. We knew he was doomed to die at any time. He died about two hours later.

16

THAILAND BY TRAIN

A couple of days after Christmas, the dream came true—we were loaded onto a train and taken south to Thailand. Some were put in boxcars, others placed on gondolas. I got on a gondola.

We left 100 Kilo Camp around ten in the morning. The sun was shining and the temperature was comfortable. The view, of course, was widespread; we were able to see everything. The only discomfort we could find was that the sparks from the wood-burning engine kept falling on us, and we had to keep a sharp lookout to keep our belongings from catching fire. By the middle of the afternoon we were in Nike Nike, Thailand, a marshaling yard and, in American terms, a division point. It was, and always had been, one of the largest camps on the line. We were scheduled to get a meal there from a Japanese kitchen, but when the men who were to carry the food to the train went to get it, there was none available. We were told that we would be at Nike Nike until some food could be prepared, which would be another two or three hours.

On the train with us was a Japanese sergeant, an engineer, who had always tried to make things as easy as he could for the Americans. He had gone to someone who was responsible for the kitchen and demanded that the food be delivered as had been arranged. We sat in the hot sun for several hours and really would have preferred to go on because the Tenth Air Force out of India had started bombing the railroad, and we figured we were in one of the prime target areas. Finally, just at dusk, we were told that the food was ready and that we could send men for it. They went and brought back several wooden tubs of clean rice and some kind of Japanese stew. We didn't know what was in it, but it was the best-tasting food we'd had in many a month.

We had all been served and the utensils had been sent back to the kitchen when a Japanese officer came along and began to question the sergeant who had been responsible for getting us a meal. Of course, we couldn't understand what was said, but it was easy to see that it concerned our food. The discussion went on for several minutes, then the officer beat the sergeant around with his saber and walked off. The sergeant was bleeding from his face when he came to our gondola and told us that he was going to have to stay in Nike Nike and that he wouldn't see us again.

We pulled out of Nike Nike about an hour after sundown. The night air was cold, and we had to open our gear to get out something to cover with. The car we were on was about ten cars behind the engine, so it was comparatively quiet. It was quiet enough for us to hear aircraft engines approaching from the north. The guard heard them too. He looked at us and said, "*Skokieda?*" We nodded, yes. He leaped up and began shouting, trying to attract the attention of some guard nearer the engine. Finally, a guard forward heard all the commotion and guessed what all the shouting was about. In a few minutes the train came to a stop. Actually, it was too late if the planes meant to use us for a target, which fortunately they didn't that night. But there were some anxious moments for the next hour and a half as the planes continued to fly over at one-minute intervals. They were B-29s on their way to Singapore.

We had one more tense situation when we crossed Wampo trestle. It was a trestle that had been built into the sheer face of a cliff that was nearly a thousand feet tall. The trestle was about halfway between top and bottom. A very narrow shelf had been made in the face of the cliff and half the track rested on it. The other side of the track was supported by pilings that were tiered up from the river bank some 500 feet or so below. It was a very flimsy-looking structure; it looked as though it might topple at any time, and we crossed it at a snail's pace. We all breathed a lot easier when the last car ran free of the trestle and the train could pick up speed again.

We arrived at the camp near what was later known as the Bridge Over the River Kwai, at Tamarkan in the middle of the morning, and some of our men were taken off there. Those who stayed on the train were scheduled to go to Nakhon Pathom, a hospital camp about twenty-five miles west of Bangkok. However, the camp was not ready to receive anyone, so we were taken off the train at Kanchanaburi and put in a small camp there that had been designated as a hospital camp.

All the men who were scheduled to go to Nakhon Pathom were supposed to be litter patients, which I was when the list was made. By the time we left 100 Kilo Camp I was ambulatory, but no change had been made regarding my status.

17

CAMP MIX-UP— KANCHANABURI, THAILAND

We thought we were in heaven at the small camp in Kanchanaburi. The huts were built of wood and the sleeping decks were wood, which was much more comfortable than bamboo had been. The food was good, the rice clean, the vegetables fresh—and there was meat and plenty of it. We had no real duty. Just police the huts and parade grounds and then we were free to do whatever we wanted to do, which wasn't much but visit with some of the other prisoners who had come from different camps—or sleep.

I was ambulatory, but the ulcer on my left shin would not heal. It continued to be an open sore covered with proud flesh, with a spot about the size of a dime that stayed black. There was always the danger that it would become active again. I had been in Kanchanaburi for a little more than a week when it was announced that the famous Dutch doctor, Dr. Henri Hekking, was coming to the camp to treat tropical ulcer cases.

Doctor Hekking's name was well known to the men of Groups 3 and 5 because he had been with Group 3 and had been responsible for the low incidence of tropical ulcers in that group. One reason for his success was that he had practiced medicine in the tropics for a number of years and had learned of different plants that grew in the jungle that had medicinal value. At the first sign of inflammation about the wound, a poultice of tea leaves would be applied. Hot water was poured over the poultice periodically. This process was continued until all signs of inflammation and infection were gone. However, if the infection did get an upper hand and the ulcer began to spread, he would use a silver spoon he had modified for the process and scoop out all the proud flesh. It was a drastic procedure, but it worked.

When it was announced that Doctor Hekking was coming to Kanchanaburi to treat ulcer patients, we also learned that he would use the "scoop out" method. All of us with ulcers were anxious—and more than a little nervous—as we stood in line in front of the hut the doctor was using for a clinic and waited for our names to be called. As each name was called, the man called would open the door and enter the hut. In just a few minutes he would come back out, sometimes walking, sometimes being carried because he had passed out during treatment. I was fifth in line and soon it came my turn.

I went into a small room and there stood the doctor and three very large Dutch orderlies. They must have weighed 300 pounds each. I was seated on a high-backed wooden chair and told to grasp my leg at the ankle and rest it on a small stool in front of the chair. There was no anesthetic available, so the patient just had to grit his teeth and hang on. The doctor made a pass through the sore and lifted out a spoonful of the proud flesh. Blood began to flow in a wide stream, and he asked me how I felt. I said, from between clenched teeth and holding a tense stomach, "It's okay. I'll make it." The blood was sopped up so the doctor could see what he had missed. He looked closely and then made another pass around the outer edge of the sore. Then the blood was sopped up once more, the open sore was packed with iodaform, and a bandage was wrapped around the wound. The doctor said for me to keep it dry and to leave the bandage in place for two weeks, but that I was to come to the clinic every day to have cod-liver oil poured on it. The rough treatment caused my leg to be sore and tender for a couple of days, but I could still walk, so it didn't bother me too much.

The hut I was assigned to held ulcer patients, and we all had received the same sort of treatment. During the first days, the odor of iodaform was overpowering. But that wasn't so bad—it was the odor of the cod-liver oil for nearly two weeks that got to us. There were more than 150 men in the hut.

About the time we were getting used to our "heaven," there being a full moon, the Tenth Air Force began to send down B-29s to carry out raids on Bangkok and Singapore. The first plane would usually arrive at Kanchanaburi about eleven at night. Then the air would be filled with the sound of B-29s until around ten o'clock the next morning. The planes would fly over at one-minute intervals, and just as the last one would be heading south the first one would be coming back going north. They were flying at 30,000 feet or more, but they were easy to see in the daylight. They looked like huge silver crosses drifting in the sky.

On one of the first fly-overs, when we had been in Kanchanaburi about two weeks, one of the planes seemed to come down unusually low. Apparently, the Japanese on the antiaircraft batteries near Tamarkan thought the pilot was going to make a bombing run because they fired on him. The sudden action took those of us in Kanchanaburi by surprise, and at first we thought the planes were bombing Tamarkan. Naturally, we thought if that was their mission, they would be over us next; so everyone ran out of the hut and got into the shallow trenches around it. Nearly everyone lay down so that all the room was taken up by the time one of the hut braggarts, a guy who said he wasn't afraid of the bombers, came out. He circled the hut a couple of times, saying, "Where can a fellow get . . . Move over . . . Oh, hell, where can a fellow get . . ." When no one would make a place for him, he said, "To hell with it," went in the hut, got in his bunk, and was asleep by the time the scare was over and we went in to go to bed.

We stayed in Kanchanaburi about six weeks, and then one day it was announced that the hospital camp at Nakhon Pathom had been completed and was ready to receive its first patients. The next morning nearly everyone in camp was taken with their gear out to the railroad tracks and put aboard the train waiting there. We traveled about two miles to the larger camp in Kanchanaburi and were told to get off. For some reason or another, there had been a mistake in the orders; we would have to stay at the large Kanchanaburi camp.

This change in plans created a chaotic condition. The large camp was not expecting us, about 500 men. They had no ready huts, no extra food, no nothing. All of a sudden 500 men had been dropped on them. To make matters worse, it began to rain. We were taken to the parade ground and told to wait while space could be found for us.

After standing in the rain for an hour, I, along with twenty-five or thirty more men, was told to follow a British sergeant-major. He would take us to a hut. He did. We went into a hut filled with Aussies, and there was not an available space to be seen. The section we were in even had tiered bunks, something that we hadn't seen before. There had always been enough space for everyone to be on the platform, which was a usual feature of all the huts we had ever been in.

The attitude of the inhabitants of this hut was not very friendly. No one offered a thing. They all stood around with a look that challenged us to open our mouths and ask for something. Finally, one Aussie took us in tow and found a space where we could put our gear down; and with a lot of crowding together, we managed to lie down. Lining up for food created the same attitude in the men there before us. We were foreigners, aliens, and no effort was spared to let us know how the regulars of the camp felt about us. Luckily, we were moved out the next day, after the orders were straightened out.

I understood later that the mix-up came when British officers in charge of designating patients for Nakhon Pathom tried to switch lists in order to get some of their officers assigned there. They had been to the camp and had seen that accommodations there were better than at any other camp they had been in; and they wanted to make sure that every "me first" British officer was first in the new camp. But the Australian officers who had made the original list won out, and those first assigned to the new camp at Nakhon Pathom got to go first.

This was but another of numerous examples of British officers' arrogant attitudes. It was an attitude that was evident much of the time, as far as the Americans and most Australians were concerned.

18

NAKHON PATHOM AND NEWS OF THE NORMANDY LANDING

We had thought that the camp at Kanchanaburi was a dream. Nakhon Pathom was paradise. The huts were brand new. They had never been used and they were spacious, as compared to the ones we had occupied in the jungle. There were large kitchen areas and latrines that could be kept clean.

The most appreciated feature was the medical clinic and hospital. The whole camp was to be regarded as a hospital, but there were special facilities for keeping bedridden patients near the clinic where they could be kept under observation of the doctors and medical orderlies. There was even a decent operating room with most of the equipment that was needed to perform surgery. Also, there was a canteen where the local Thais could bring their goods and sell to the prisoners. It seemed this was going to be a great place to recuperate from all the illnesses that had been so overpowering in the jungle. And, for the most part, it worked out that way.

I had been there but a couple of days before I was assigned to a task, as were all ambulatory patients. I was made a member of a litter-bearer team. The system was devised whereby all patients suffering the same illness were put in one particular hut, which served as a ward would in a regular hospital. A record was kept on each man, listing his ailment and prescribed treatment. If he required surgery or some type of examination, his name was given to a team of litter bearers. They went to his hut, picked him up, delivered him to the clinic, waited on him, and returned him to his hut when his visit with the doctor was finished. Usually, my team would make eight or ten trips a day. There were four other teams and their schedule was about the same as ours. To supplement the staff working in the clinic, a team of traveling medics was organized. These men went from hut to hut dispensing various types of medication because now, here in Nakhon Pathom, we were beginning to get some drugs.

Food was exceptionally good. In just a few weeks everyone was putting on weight, and most of the illnesses caused by malnutrition were showing signs of moderating. This was about May of 1944.

I was in this hospital when the landing at Normandy took place. We got news of it just a few hours after it began. I would never forget that day.

The hospital camp was only a mile or so from a Thai Air Force base. On D-day, though we hadn't been told the news yet, a flight of B-29s was heard above the clouds at Nakhon Pathom. Very soon after the first plane had passed over, there was a great deal of activity on the Thai air base; and in a little while we heard the bee-like buzz of airplane motors and then saw three small Italian-made biplanes take off and climb over the clouds.

We could hear the solid resonating hum of the B-29 engines, a deep bass sort of a hum, and we could hear the high bee-like buzz of the Thai airplanes. Then there was a *whump. . . whump . . . whump . . .* of the twenty-millimeter cannons aboard the B-29s and a *tat . . . tat . . . tat . . . tat . . .* of the small machine guns on the Thai planes, followed by a couple more *whump . . . whumps.* And then, without interruption, there was the high-pitched hum of a plane in a dive. As we looked in the direction of the sounds, we saw one of the biplanes break through the clouds, smoke streaming from the fuselage and heading for the landing strip. It was followed by the other two planes, which landed as soon as they could. We cheered and felt like we were on the winning side—for a change. About an hour later we were told that the allies had landed on Normandy. We began counting the days, but there were to be more than several before we were actually liberated.

19

TAMARKAN, THAILAND— HAVEN FOR BLACK MARKETEERS

I stayed in Nakhon Pathom for about six weeks and then was sent to Tamarkan, one of the large base camps in Thailand. The camp at Tamarkan was located on the bank of the Mae Khlong River, just below its confluence with the Khwae Noi River—the site of the aforementioned notorious Bridge Over the River Kwai. Tamarkan was by this time a well-organized camp. Most all the inmates were regaining their health, and many profitable rackets flourished among the prisoners.

Ever since the Japanese had taken their first prisoner of war, there had been a few hardy souls who were enterprising enough to want to make a buck, wanted to beat the system, or just wanted the excitement of outwitting someone. They were called black marketeers. They would buy, or in some cases steal, a valuable item from another prisoner and then would, in most cases, go outside the camp and deal with the local population. Valuable items included a pair of trousers in reasonably good condition, a blanket, a pair of boots that had not been worn because the owner hadn't wanted to mess them up (he was probably saving them for the really hard times), a watch, a fountain pen, a mechanical pencil, a wedding ring, a gold tooth pulled out so it could be converted to cash. Just about anything was valuable. In Tamarkan a good pair of khaki trousers would bring the prisoner twenty *ticals* (Thai dollars). The black marketeer would get sixty for them outside the camp. A good blanket would go for forty in the camp, one hundred outside. Many people, mostly British officers, denounced these people as racketeers, but my view was that they were responsible for keeping the economy in the camp at a high level. Money was fairly easy to come by if a fellow could be enterprising enough. This would not have been possible if the camps had to depend on the comparatively small amount of money that was introduced into the economy by the pay the Japanese put out.

Some people formed combines and manufactured cigarettes, clogs, spoons, and candies and cakes. I took up the tailor trade. I would make a pair of trousers for twenty-five dollars, the buyer supplying the material. I cut hair, as I had done in Batavia. But here the price had gone up: two dollars for a haircut, two dollars for a shave. I never did have the nerve to take up the black market trade. I left that to those who were more daring— or more foolish. I never could really decide which they were.

20

KHON KHAN, THAILAND

By March of 1944, with the railroad in operation, the Japanese began to set up small maintenance camps of about 200 men each at fifty-kilometer intervals all along the railroad from Chungkai to Thanbyuzayat. It was late June when I got in Tamarkan, and I stayed only a couple of weeks before I was named on a draft to go to one of these camps. There were one hundred Dutchmen, ninety-seven Australians, two British, and one American—me.

We were sent to a camp at a place named Khon Khan. It was a sort of division point on the railroad, about fifty kilometers south of Nike Nike. It was located about two hundred yards from the river and was right next to the tracks and a siding. The guards were Japanese engineers, a couple of squads of them (an American squad is sixteen men). The officer in charge was Captain Suzuki, the only officer whose name I knew.

Our task, in addition to repairing minor bomb damage to the railroad, was to reopen a communication road that the British had used in the 1930s to get from Malaya to Rangoon. The road ran through the mountains; and because it hadn't been used for years, the jungle was taking over. Nevertheless, most of the roadbed was still visible. Also, many of the bridges were still in place, but they had to be rebuilt because they were rotted out. Some of the British troops who had worked on the

134

railroad in that area had built a bridge across the Khwae Noi at that point and had cleared the roadbed some five miles or so into the jungle. Our first task was to go a couple of miles beyond the cleared portion and construct a drainage system in a bog and swamp area—then working back toward the cleared road, rebuild a couple of bridges and clear the trees off the roadbed. We were to live in the jungle for five days, come into camp for a couple of days, then go back to the jungle again—sort of a routine. And that is what we did.

The bog and swamp we were to drain was approximately a quarter of a mile long. We dug a ditch about three feet deep on either side of the strip that was to be used for the roadbed and then dug lateral ditches off to one side into the jungle. Next we placed two layers of three- and four-inch saplings, wired together, over the mud. On top of the sapling mats, we put a six-inch layer of gravel for the riding surface. The job took about three weeks. As we were trying to dig the ditches, we were continually disturbed by truckloads of Japanese troops headed north to Burma. We had to stop our work many times and pull the trucks through the muddy bog.

My stay at Khon Khan lasted for about six months, and some interesting things took place during that time. One of the first things happened when we went into the jungle to rebuild the communication road. We went out to the site where the roadbed was going to have to be cleared and a bridge rebuilt before we could take trucks any farther into the mountains. This work would require that we camp in the open for a couple of nights, so the engineers set up a camp area in one part of a grove of trees. We prisoners set up our camp over just a bit from the Japanese, with a few clumps of underbrush between us and them. On the second evening as we were having supper, we heard a loud scream followed by a lot of commotion with engineers running every which way. We raised up so that we could see over the underbrush and there, standing beside the stew pot which had been set in the middle of all the engineers, was the man who had done the cooking that day. He was laughing so hard he could barely stand up. In a few minutes, after everyone had come back to the camp area, the sergeant of the engineers told us what had happened. The cook had killed a monkey. He had cut it up and put the meat in the stew. And he had put the head in the stew without cleaning it. One of the engineers had dipped the ladle deep into the pot and brought it up with the monkey staring at him. That was when all the engineers ran out, and supper was definitely over.

After we had cleared the road and rebuilt the bridge, we were able to go deeper into the mountains. One day we had been cutting trees and brush out of the roadway, and by the end of the day our trucks were parked at the top of a fairly steep hill. At the bottom of the hill was a narrow creek with a bridge over it. The usual signal was given for everyone to load into the trucks and start for camp. I was in the second truck in the line, and we watched as the first truck started to coast down the hill. The driver couldn't start the truck, so he was going to let it coast down the hill to get the motor started. As he neared the bridge he lost control and the truck's left wheels missed the bridge. The truck fell to the left. Luckily, there were some tall trees to hold it on the road, but the thirty men who had been in the bed of the truck were scattered along the road and down in the creek. Fortunately, no one was killed. One Aussie suffered a broken arm, several had some bad lacerations, and a couple of the Japanese got scratched up. Captain Suzuki worked the driver over pretty good; he looked nearly as bad as the ones who were injured in the wreck.

We had worked on the communication road during June, July, and August of 1944. We had reconstructed some ten or twelve miles of the road and had built a fancy bridge just north of the camp that crossed a slough that ran to the river. Other camps had made the road usable on each side of Khon Khan and the Japanese were running trucks over it every day. So with the communication road in operation, it was decided that we would cut firewood for the railroad engines and stack it alongside the tracks. We cut down trees either side of the tracks and then cut the trunks into lengths about two feet long and stacked them near the right-of-way.

One afternoon we had just gone up a little rise a few hundred feet from the right-of-way to start cutting down a tree when we heard the unmistakable sound of B-24 bomber engines. We looked up and to our right, and there—just a couple of miles away—were three B-24s flying very low, at about a thousand feet or less. They had just come over the top of the hill, and we couldn't hear them until they got on our side. They flew off to the south about five miles and then circled and started heading in our direction.

I was with my British buddy, and we figured we'd be okay since we were not near anything that could be regarded as a target; so we just stood still and watched. About the time we estimated that the planes were over our camp, some three miles down from us, we saw the streaks of bombs falling from the bomb bays. A few seconds of silence followed, then a sharp, staccato sound as the bombs exploded. In another few minutes, a huge cloud of dust flew up in the air. We agreed that our camp had been wiped out and thanked our lucky stars that we had not been there. The bombers flew over our heads and continued flying north over the hill.

All was quiet for several minutes, and then we heard Captain Suzuki calling for everyone to assemble on the road to our left. We could see guys coming out of the brush all around and were about to go down ourselves when the sound of the bomber motors could be heard again. We looked up and the planes were coming in from the west at about 500 feet. We ran to the river, splashed to a sandbar, and dived under some scrubby brush that grew there in the dry season. A Burmese boy about fourteen years old was following us. We hoped that the bombardiers would have no reason to drop bombs on a small sandbar in the middle of a river. We had just crouched down and turned to get our eyes on the planes when we heard a strange sound—a sort of whining punctuated with huffs and puffs. We looked to our right and saw sand flying into the air. It was the Burmese boy. In less than half a minute he had dug a hole in the sand deep enough for him to be below ground level—and was still digging. Despite our present fright, we had to burst out laughing. The sight of his saucerlike eyes brought on another outburst of laughter. This one was cut short, though, when we heard a sound that was strange to us. It was partly a whistle and partly the sound of a jet. We looked up just in time to see three rather long, black objects streaking away from the bomb bays of one of the planes. They formed an almost perfect triangle, and the rear end of each object was glowing like a tracer bullet. A trail of brown smoke marked their course from the plane. The three objects went out of sight as they fell below the level of the road, and we heard a muffled *whump!* as they exploded. My British buddy said, "They must have been duds." I agreed, for there wasn't that much noise.

We stayed under the brush on the sandbar until we heard Captain Suzuki and the guards calling for us to come up on the road. We went across the dry riverbed, climbed up the small bluff to the road, and were amazed at what we saw just across the road. There before us, where just a few minutes before had been three bamboo huts, was an oval-shaped hole twenty feet deep and about one hundred feet on the long dimension and fifty feet on the short dimension.

All the work detail lined up in the road to be counted. Captain Suzuki determined that three prisoners were missing. Someone spoke up and said that he had seen some guys running for the huts just before the bombs had been dropped; so Captain Suzuki said that we were to go over to the hole and see if we could find any remains of the guys who were thought to have been in the huts. We walked back and forth, to and fro, but couldn't find any trace of blood, skin, or bones. After about an hour of searching, it was finally concluded that the bombs had done a thorough job of grinding up and burying our fellow prisoners. Although the sun was still fairly high in the sky, Captain Suzuki called it a day and we returned to camp.

We really expected to find that our huts had been demolished; however, when we came around the curve in the road just to the north of the camp, we saw our huts and the guardhouse all standing and intact. The guys who had been in camp were anxious to learn what had happened where we had been, and we were anxious to learn what had happened when the bombs fell so near our camp. There was a hubbub of voices for a few minutes. Then, by a process of elimination, it was determined who the missing men were. Everyone felt a deep sense of sadness that three Australians who suffered and survived the rigors of the camps through the rainy season had finally been done in by some of their own people. The bombs that had fallen near our camp had been antipersonnel bombs, and they had all but demolished a civilian labor camp a half mile to the south of our camp. Of the 2,000 Tamils and Malays who were in the camp, 700 had been killed outright, and nearly all the others were injured. The Japanese just let the bodies lay where they had fallen, and vultures were in the air for days afterwards.

The atmosphere of sadness continued as we ate our evening meal. Everyone found an excuse to turn in early, not wanting to talk about the loss we had suffered with the three Australians. The camp was quiet at about eleven o'clock when voices could be heard singing the Australian national anthem, "Bless 'Em All." Three guards dashed from the guardhouse, ran around our hut, and made it clear that none of us was to come out. Captain Suzuki ran out shouting orders, and the engineers in their G-strings grabbed their rifles and ducked behind the guardhouse to wait for the owners of the voices to come down the road. As they came into view in the light of a half moon, Captain Suzuki stepped out from behind the guardhouse and challenged the men on the road. After a little confusion, it was discovered that they were the three missing Aussies.

The men said that when the bombers came over, they did start to go into one of the huts. Then they remembered that until just a day or two before, the huts had held a large cache of gasoline drums, so they decided to keep going down the road. They had gone around a curve and had spotted a Burmese "beer-joint" setting in the jungle at the side of the road. They went in and got to talking with the Burmese in the place and had a few drinks. The next thing they knew it was dark; so they decided that maybe they should go back to camp.

There was no punishment or reprimand; Captain Suzuki actually seemed happy to see that the Aussies were still alive. He had been very concerned when they couldn't be found. On more than one occasion he had shown that he had humane feelings toward us prisoners.

It was late in the fall of 1944 that American and British troops were dealing the Japanese a lot of misery in northern Burma. Almost every night trains loaded with guns and troops would pass the camp going north. Then in the daylight hours they would be headed south with wounded and sick. On several occasions a train loaded with wounded stopped on the siding at

Khon Khan, and those who were able would walk down to the river and bathe and wash clothes. We had been told that we were not to talk to the soldiers or to in any other way have any contact with them. But it happened one day that just at noon, while we were having our noon meal in camp, a train pulled onto the siding and Japanese soldiers came off it in droves to go to the river. My British buddy and I, more out of curiosity than for any other reason, went over to one of the cars and glanced in the open door. As we stood there we heard a whisper of a voice saying, "Can you help me? Would you help me, please?" We had been warned repeatedly about having contact with these people, but what were we to do? Just ignore someone in trouble? We looked at each other. Then, without saying a word, we leaped up into the car and went back and picked up the man and carried him to the door. We carried him on down to the river, expecting any minute to have a guard or Captain Suzuki jump us and bash us around; however, everyone ignored us, even though we were in plain view.

As we helped the man wash some of the filth off his face and body, he told us that he was an army captain and that he had been fighting in north Burma. He said that the Americans had begun to use unfair tactics: They would send in tanks with flame throwers and burn all the brush and trees, then the tanks would pull out and infantrymen would rush in, each with an automatic rifle or machine gun, and fire at anything that moved. The Japanese could only move at night, and then they had to be very careful. He said it was a totally unfair way to fight a war. We thought it was not the time or place to remind him of Pearl Harbor, the Philippines, Hong Kong, Singapore, or Java, but the thoughts of these places ran through our minds as we carried him back to the boxcar. Not one of his buddies offered to help him after we had gotten him to the water. It amazed us that men could be so unmindful of their own kind. Yet we saw example after example of this kind of "military courtesy" or "honor" among the Japanese troops.

We spent Christmas of 1944 in Khon Khan. And though the Japanese army did not recognize Christmas, Captain Suzuki did allow us to have a *yasemae* day on that day. As we were celebrating with some homemade *saki* that night, a couple of the guards joined us and got just as drunk as we did.

Before the civilian labor camp had been bombed, a couple of the Aussies had sneaked down there and had some black-market dealings with some of the Tamils. One time in the course of their business, they had asked for and received a recipe for brewing *saki*. So all during the months of November and December, they had a crock of the drink brewing in one corner of the hut. They would taste it from time to time, but they were saving it for the Christmas celebration, should we be allowed to have one.

We waited until after dark to pass the brew around; then just five guys at a time would go in the hut, get a portion in a cup, sip it, and then come out. Alas, unnoticed by us, one of the guards became curious about the way the men seemed to be going into the hut in groups, so he decided to investigate. He investigated just when it was time for me and my British buddy to go in. We went to the back of the hut, climbed up on the platform, and a few drops of the *saki* was poured in our cups. We had just taken a little sip when the call, "*Kioski!*" (attention) was yelled out at the door. We couldn't scatter, for that would surely look suspicious, so we grabbed up some cards and tried to pretend that we were playing cards. The guard didn't go for that because he had seen us just enter the hut. He couldn't speak English, but he could make us understand, by using the mixture of English-Malay-Japanese language that had developed in all the camps, that he knew something was going on and that he wanted to know what it was.

He pointed at a cup and wanted to know what was in it. We told him it was water. He indicated that he wanted to taste it. The attitude by that time was, "What the hell, he knows something's up, so give him a shot." He took a little sip, and it didn't take a connoisseur to tell it wasn't water. "Ah so, *sakika. Bagoose* (very good). *Nandaka* (where is it)?" The owners of the crock showed it to him; it was still more than half full. The guard then indicated that he wanted someone to keep a lookout for the sergeant, laid his rifle on the platform, and crawled up and crossed his legs as he joined us. The conversation, held in the mixture of languages, was the usual: about families, hometowns, and Japan winning the war. After a few fairly hefty swallows, the guard was beginning to get tipsy. He realized it, and said he had better go. He left and in a few minutes another guard showed up at the door of the hut. It was evident from the way he was acting that he knew what was what, so he was let in the back of the hut to get his share. He went back to the guardhouse after fifteen or twenty minutes feeling pretty good.

The Japanese did celebrate New Year's Day; so we got another *yasemae* day then, and a few bottles of real Japanese *saki* were passed around. Shortly after the new year of 1945 got under way, word came to the Japanese that a graves commission from Switzerland, presumably connected with the International Red Cross, was going to be in Burma and Thailand to inspect the cemeteries that had been established at the railroad camps. As a result of this alert, a cemetery clean-up detail was put together; it included me, one Dutchman, one Australian, and my British buddy. We were told to get enough gear together so that we would have a bed and eating utensils. We would be gone from Khon Khan for a week or two, but would return there. No details of what the job was to be would be given until we got under way. We were told all of this one night, and the next morning we had everything ready.

Just after the morning *tanko* (muster), a track inspector's car was at the camp to pick up us prisoners and two Japanese guards. The inspector's car was a small trolleylike vehicle that had four bench-type seats (two, back-to-back) and could carry as many as twelve passengers plus the operator. With just six passengers, we had room to pack our gear on a couple of the seats and ride in comparative comfort. After we had gone a couple of miles from the camp, one of the guards told us what our job was to be. We felt there was a certain amount of honor in the job, but were sorry that it had to be done. We went north from Khon Khan. Presumably, someone else was going to take care of the cemeteries to the south; but I never met another ex-POW who was aware or ever heard of this particular operation. In any event, the story of the Swiss commission is what we were told.

We started at Nike Nike and were able to get one cemetery cleaned up each day. There was no "*speedo*" about it. We just worked at a steady pace; and when it got dark, guards and prisoners cooked the evening meal, talked awhile, and went to bed.

In the morning we would move on to the next cemetery. Naturally, I was especially interested in 100 Kilo Camp, and when we reached it I didn't recognize anything. All the huts had been taken away and the jungle had done a good job of reclaiming the area. It had been nearly a year to the day since I had last seen the camp area. The only way I was able to get my bearings was from a large stump that had stood just outside our hut. I found the stump, but still had trouble picturing the location of the different huts as they had been when we were in the camp.

The cemetery was in terrible shape. It was on the side of a hill, and we found that some of the graves had been washed away so that the bones of the men who had been buried there were lying in a small ravine that had washed out on one side of the cemetery. We collected as many of the bones as we could find, reburied them, and cleaned out all the undergrowth and vines—just as we had at all the other cemeteries.

Most of the rest of the time was uneventful, but the night we spent at the 105 Kilo Camp was exciting for a while. We had finished at 100 Kilo Camp just before sundown, so the guard suggested that we go on over to 105 Kilo Camp because there were some huts still standing there that would offer a little shelter in case it should rain. Furthermore, that was where we were going to work the next day. So to 105 we went. We had just gotten there and parked the trolley on a little spur line when we heard airplane motors. We looked out over the river to the northwest and saw three B-24s flying pretty low in our direction. At the same time, a train was coming from the south, shooting sparks fifty feet in the air as it pulled up the slight grade just south of 105 Kilo Camp. One of the guards yelled, "*Skoki!*" (aircraft) and began to run toward the river. The other guard was right behind him, and we prisoners were strung out behind him. I think we prisoners got to the river bank first, but it really didn't matter. It wasn't a race to see who could win. It was a race to stay alive. We were sure the planes would bomb the train and we wanted to be as far away as possible.

The planes continued in our direction. They passed right over the train, which was loaded with ammunition and gasoline, without dropping anything and continued on a straight course until they were out of sight. We stayed down on the river bank for about an hour, but never saw or heard the planes again. However, a little after midnight there was another scare and another race for the river bank when we heard motors again. This time they were from a mission that was flying south to Bangkok, and the planes made no move to alter their 30,000-foot height.

On one *yasemae* day while we were at 105 Kilo, I climbed a high hill just across the railroad tracks and spent the whole afternoon on the side opposite the camp watching—and envying—a couple of hawks circling the valley, and thinking of home and my family and wishing the war would end so that I could get back to them. Usually on *yasemae* day we would go with the guards and dynamite fish in the river. It was the dry season and the river was low; one could walk across the cold water. It was only about five feet at the deepest point, but it got pretty wide, maybe a thousand feet, more or less. The guards would go upstream about a quarter of a mile and throw in plugs of dynamite. We would stand downstream and collect all the stunned fish until the guards ran out of dynamite; then the fish would be divided among all present.

The cemetery-cleaning detail was finished in about ten days, and it was sometime in February 1945 when we were taken south again. Chungkai was a new camp for me, but some of the Aussies had been there before. After we got there, my British buddy ran into one of his army buddies and moved into his hut. I then buddied up with an Aussie I had been friends with at Khon Khan.

21

CHUNGKAI, THAILAND— AMERICANS BOMB THE BRIDGE

Chungkai was a real rest camp by the time I got there. Most camp duties were assigned on rotation, and it was nearly a month before I was given anything to do. Most of my time was spent roaming from hut to hut, having conversations with the Aussies. There weren't many Americans there, and the ones that were participated in the black-market business and had a clique of their own; so I was left pretty much to myself as a "Yank." Finally, I was assigned to the garden detail. A camp garden had been made that supplied most of the fresh vegetables for the camp, and I got the job of weeding it and hauling water.

There was another garden there which belonged to the officers—a typical British officer idea. They thought of themselves as being too far above ordinary ranks, as they called enlisted men, to eat from the same garden, so they were given the privilege of having a separate area to raise their vegetables. Their garden was right in the center of the enlisted men's huts—as a show, I always thought—and seemed to be an attempt to shove their arrogance down the ordinary rank's throats. The garden was patrolled day and night by MPs, which presented a real challenge to steal from it. It could be and was done, but it wasn't easy. Nevertheless, an occasional theft did serve to keep the hated MPs on their toes. The favorite name for the MPs was "Gestapo."

145

Shortly after I had been assigned to the garden crew, I came down with malaria. I was fortunate, for by that time the camps had begun to get medical supplies and Chungkai had a good supply of quinine. I was put in the hospital and began taking the bitter medicine. A patient had two choices: He could have the dose of quinine either in liquid form with half a lemon as a chaser, or in capsule form, chased by half a boiled egg. I chose the capsule form. The capsule itself was made up of rice paper, and it worked well if a man could swallow fast; otherwise, the paper would come apart and the bitter taste of quinine would linger for hours. It made me deathly sick to get the powdered quinine spread about in my mouth. The liquid I just couldn't do at all. About five minutes after taking a dose, which I think was about twenty grains, I would get a headache and my vision would become blurred. It was a lot like having a hangover, but worse. That condition would last about three hours, then on the fourth hour I would get another dose. I would try to eat during the hour I felt like I might live, because it was impossible to eat with the quinine hangover.

Even though the quinine supply was coming in, men continued to die of blackwater fever. Blackwater fever was the acute stage of malaria and was characterized by the urine being black because of blood in it. To die of blackwater fever was to die a very agonizing death. Every day or two a patient would be carried to one end of the hut where all blackwater patients were taken. Once a man got the disease, there was nothing that could be done for him except to let him die. Once in a while a man would recover from it, but it was a rare occurrence. Sometimes I found it difficult to sleep at night because when everything was quiet, I could hear the men in the blackwater fever end of the hut moaning and crying; and there was nothing anyone could do for them.

I was in the hospital about two weeks with the bout of malaria. When I was released I had lost about twenty pounds, and my Aussie buddy wanted to help me gain it back. Through a connection or two that he had, he got me a job as batman to an Australian captain. I told him I didn't think I would work out on the job, but he insisted that there wasn't a lot to it. Just keep the captain's quarters clean, do his laundry—in general, serve as a valet to the man. I lasted less than a week. I had gone down and gotten the captain's breakfast one morning, and when I returned to the hut he began to complain that I had been too slow. I told him he was welcome to stand in the line because I was through, and walked out. The job ran against my grain anyway. I just couldn't get over a man being tended to in a POW camp, especially after having been through the jungle camps and having seen my shipmates die so needlessly because they couldn't be tended to when they really needed it.

A day or two after that I came down with dengue fever. I woke up one morning with a headache and feeling terrible. It seemed like all my joints ached. I told my Aussie buddy that I was going to miss breakfast that morning but that I wished he would bring me a cup of tea when he came back. By the time he returned, I was having a chill that made a malaria chill seem mild. The freezing and shivering lasted about an hour, and then I began to have a fever and ached in every joint and fiber of my body. I couldn't bear lying down. I couldn't stand on my feet. Even the slightest noise made it seem that my head would split apart. My buddy brought me a cup of hot tea and I managed to get it down. In fact, that was what I lived on for the next ten days. About four times a day, especially when I was having the chills, he would get me a quart of boiling hot tea. I would drink it as quickly as I could for the warm liquid seemed to reduce the coldness of the chill. Then I would lie down and he would pile blankets and a couple of overcoats on me and I'd sweat a few gallons. The memory of those ten days was hazy at the time and really didn't get a lot better over the years. It was one of the most miserable periods of my life.

It was near the end of the siege, probably on the eighth day or so, that I began to feel that I might live. I could now sit up for thirty minutes to an hour without aching all over. It was in the afternoon and my buddy had gone to the river to bathe. All of a sudden there was the sound of loud, excited talk outside the hut and then the noisy roar of aircraft engines, which sounded as though they were in the hut with us. Next came a loud *rat-a-tat-tat!* of a machine gun. Then everyone was running out of the hut. I tried to get someone to tell me what was going on, but everyone was too excited and in a hurry to get outside. I was too weak to

walk, so for a little while I just had to sit and listen to the talk. I
heard those outside say, "Oh look how low they are . . . they look
like Yanks. See the markings." About this time my Aussie buddy
came in and said, "Hey, Tex, we'd better get out and see the show.
Some of your blokes are up there having a look around. They just
flew down the river and cleared their guns and I got one of the
casings." He shoved a brass shell in my hand as he grabbed me
under a shoulder, and we ran for the door because we could hear
an airplane coming over again.

We ran out the door just in time to look up and see a B-24
not more than 200 feet over us. It seemed like we could reach up
and touch it as it passed over our heads. We could even see two
guys standing in the bomb bay doors, waving. The plane went
over the trees on the river bank and dipped down. In just a short
while we saw it climbing for altitude a couple of miles out. We kept
watching the plane as it went to about 2,000 feet and then turned
to line up on the Bridge Over the River Kwai. In the meantime,
three other planes had performed a glide bomb run on the
bridge, and then the one we had been watching did the same
thing. The plane got to a thousand feet, then went into a long
glide. We could see the bomb tumble from the bomb bay and in
a few seconds smoke and dirt shot up into the air, followed by the
sound of a loud explosion. The plane made another pass over
camp and then flew to the west and went out of sight.

The whole show had lasted nearly a half hour; and by the
time the planes left, the Japanese guards were ripping and raging
through the camp. They ran everyone into the huts and stood
outside pointing their rifles about and acting as if they were going
to pull the trigger just any time. Everyone had to stay in the huts
that night; but we had plenty to talk about, so it really didn't matter. Except that it was awfully hot, and my head was about to blow
off after all the excitement died down.

A few days before the spectacular bombing raid on the
bridge, a project was started in Chungkai that raised questions
but got no definite answers. Work details were organized to begin digging a moat around the camp. This big ditch was twelve
feet wide and six feet deep. The question was: Was the purpose
of the moat to keep the prisoners in the camp? Or was it to bury
them in if the fighting war reached Thailand? The Japanese

would give no answers. One strong rumor that circulated at the time, and one that was accepted by most everyone, was that the moat was being dug to keep the black marketeers in camp. Black marketing had become so popular that as many as thirty-five to forty people, maybe more, were leaving camp every night to go out and trade with the local Thais and Chinese. Whatever the reason for the moat, I was never to find out, because I was sent to another camp before it was finished.

22

SMALL CAMP ON A THAI FARM— WAR NEWS BAD FOR THE ENEMY

Around the last of May 1945, I went to the smallest camp I was ever to be in. Again, I was the only American. The camp had approximately fifty or sixty Australians, fifteen or so Dutch, a few British, and me—the lone American.

We were made up into a work detail one day and sent to a very small campsite about ten miles east of Nakhon Pathom, or fifteen miles west of Bangkok. The huts were on the private property of a Thai rice farmer. The Japanese had gone in and commandeered enough of his land to build three small huts and a tool shed. Prisoners occupied one hut, Japanese guards occupied one, and one was used as a kitchen to prepare food for both the guards and the prisoners.

The Thai farmer's property was an area of some twenty acres that had trees on it and, as is usual all over Thailand, was completely surrounded by his rice paddies. The camp was about a quarter of a mile from the road that ran between Nakhon Pathom and Bangkok, which had the railroad running beside it, which in turn had the canal running beside it. In other words, there were three means of transportation that ran from Nakhon Pathom to Bangkok just across a rice paddy from the camp—by vehicle, by train, or by boat. About a mile and a half east of the camp was a narrow river that had a bridge over it, and sometime in early April the bridge had been damaged by bombs. Since the

Japanese by that time had neither the material nor the time to repair it, they took us prisoners there to operate a system so that they could run the trains out of Bangkok to the bridge. We laid tracks alongside the approach to the bridge, where the side track ran on a rather steep grade right down to the water's edge. We would take three cars at a time down this track, unload them, and put the cargo on a ferry to cross the river. Then on the other side of the river, we would unload the ferry and load all the cargo into a train waiting to go north. Trains coming from the north were loaded with sick and wounded; and as the order had been in Khon Khan, we were not to communicate or in any other way have any contact with these troops.

The routine of the camp was really informal, even more than it had been in Khon Khan. The only commissioned officer we had was a young lieutenant. He was probably about twenty or twenty-two. He was taller than the average Japanese and was very smart in all his actions, very military. But he was humane and not really a slave driver and, as far as I was ever able to determine, had no personal axe to grind. He never caused a prisoner to be intentionally mistreated, as far as I knew.

The job site being where it was put us in close proximity to Thai nationals, because passengers on the train out of Bangkok had to walk down the tracks we laid in order to get to the ferry themselves. So at least a couple of times a day, Thai civilians would be walking right in our midst. As with any other commuter service, here were people whom we came to recognize as regular travelers on the train. One I remembered especially was a middle-aged Chinese man. Whenever he came through, he would drop one- and five-*tical* bills near a prisoner if no guard was looking. He always smiled and nodded his head in a friendly greeting. Some of the Thais did the same thing.

One day we were moving a set of three boxcars down a ramplike affair. We used railroad ties across the tracks to keep the cars from moving too fast. Somehow or another the ties we had in place became dislodged and the cars sped down the ramp, jumped off the track, crashed into three Thai sampans which always were tied to the ferry landing, and disappeared under the water. Seven Thais were killed and their sampans were sunk. That didn't do much to endear the Japanese to the Thai people in the community; and about a week later, a Japanese private on his way back from the job site was waylaid in a brushy spot just outside of the camp. He was pretty well beaten up and his rifle was stolen. The assault took place within earshot of the Japanese hut; so from then on the guards always traveled in twos and threes.

It was really pitiful to see a train loaded with wounded come in. It was every man for himself. Even if the poor guy was weak from malaria or dysentery or had half his head shot off, he had to carry his own gear and make his own way. Some of the time they would have to wait for the train to come out from Bangkok; and while they waited, they would sit under the trees on the side of the river where we had put up a shelter. Usually we would try to give them water or a little food if they seemed to want it.

One day I was walking around a group of about twelve soldiers who had just come in on one train and were waiting for the train to Bangkok. I was passing about three or four feet from them when one of them said, "Can you get me a cigarette?" I looked around and saw that the fellow speaking was fairly young. His English was perfect. I rolled a cigarette and the next time I passed him, I dropped it near him. I made another round and he asked for a light. I glanced around and saw that our guards were busy down by the river, so I kneeled down and struck the lighter I had and held it to the cigarette. After he got it going he said, "Thanks. In a few weeks our positions will be reversed." I didn't think I understood him so I gave him a questioning look. He said, "In a few weeks you will be the guards and we will be the prisoners. Things are very bad for us. I am not a soldier; I am a newspaper correspondent and I have heard the news of the war. Japan is losing and it will all be over in a few weeks." He wrote his address on a pad as he spoke, and after he had finished telling me about how the war was going, he handed me the piece of paper and said, "This is my address. Will you write to me after you get home again?" I took the paper and moved away feeling encouraged.

We had been getting news of what was going on in the Pacific nearly from the first day we had been at this small camp. I suppose we had been on the job at the bridge about three days when one morning we heard the deep drone of an aircraft engine. We looked up just as a B-24 flew over our heads at about

3,000 feet altitude. The plane was so close by the time we heard it that we suspected that it had glided in, and that we had only heard it when the pilot revved up the motor to make a turn. As the noise of the motor was roaring around us, I glanced at the Japanese officer who made a hand signal that we were to run into the trees and get away from the bridge. We all thought the bridge was going to be bombed again because we looked up as we ran and saw two large objects falling from the plane. Just as we hit the ground, the objects exploded in the sky and thousands of leaflets began to fall. The sky resembled a tiny snowstorm for a while. As soon as the Japanese officer realized what was happening, he called all us prisoners together and made us sit down until all the leaflets hit the ground. Several of them had drifted near us, but the guards grabbed them up and stuffed them in their pockets.

The next day one of the train passengers who had to walk past us handed one of our guys one of the leaflets. It was printed in Siamese, but it had the English translation written between the lines. Also, there were pictures of some of the action on Saipan, a place we had never heard of, and a picture of the landing force that had taken part in the landing there. We couldn't believe that America had so many ships in one operation.

The same plane would drop leaflets every Wednesday, and on Thursday we would get the translated version. Sometimes we would get it from a passenger on the train; other times it would be from one of the coolies working in the rice warehouse near the river. One time the farmer whose land we were on brought a copy at night after the Japanese had gone to sleep.

23

THE WAR IS OVER—
HOME AGAIN AT LAST

About the first of August 1945, our routine changed. Only about half of the men in the camp went to work on the ferry and railroad; the other half were put to work building a sort of revetment in the rice paddy to the east side of the camp. We cut blocks of sod out of the paddy and stacked them up in bricklike fashion to form a wall about six feet high. The wall was battered, or tapered. It was wider at the bottom than it was at the top. An areaway between the walls was about four feet wide, and the fortification was about one hundred feet long. On each end was a circular shape that was to be used as a machine-gun position. Our guess was that we were building a defense position to repel paratroopers. We never did get to find out.

We had the thing almost complete when one day we went to our hut, as was usual, for lunch. The only thing unusual about it was that the guys working on the railroad had been brought in. We didn't think a lot about it because it was impossible to ever guess what the Japanese had in mind. We ate our lunch and took a short nap, which was also usual since this camp was very informal and we weren't driven all that hard. At any rate, we had the nap and were expecting the Japanese sergeant to come get us and take us to the tool shed to get our tools so we could go back to work. We waited . . . one-thirty . . . two o'clock . . . three o'clock in the afternoon—still no sergeant. No sign of any

154

Japanese. We began to get a little uneasy because we thought they might be waiting for nighttime and then would shoot us. One wild guess was that the war was over, but the guy who suggested that was laughed down.

Finally, just as it was getting dark enough that we were going to have to light a lamp so we could see what we were doing, we saw a procession coming up the road about a quarter of a mile across the rice paddy. Someone said, "Hey! Listen! They're singing!" Everyone got silent because very often Thai children would walk around at night singing, and they did make beautiful music. "Hey, that's not Thais. They're singing 'She'll Be Comin' 'Round the Mountain'," said a voice in the dark.

The group we saw was carrying torches; and as we watched, the torch carriers turned in on the path that would bring them into our camp. "Hey! What the hell's going on?" someone wanted to know. We were transfixed as the group of ten or twelve came nearer. Then one of them called out, "Any Aussies here?"

"Yeah, mate. What's up?" asked someone from our hut.

"The war's over," came a reply. "We were at a little camp just up the road, and the Jap officer up there told us that you guys were down here and told us to come down here and join you. They're gonna send trucks down to pick us up in the morning and take us to Nakhon Pathom," a self-appointed spokesman for the group said.

"Would you say that again, mate?" said an Aussie in our group.

"The bloody war's over, mate. We talked to a truck driver from Nakhon Pathom this afternoon, and he said they had gone crazy up there. Said there were all the allies' flags flyin' over the main gate and all the Jap guards had been locked up in a couple of the huts and all. . . The f—— war's really over!" the spokesman declared.

We couldn't believe the war was really over, but cautiously we began to talk about it. True or not, we hadn't had a subject this exciting to talk about in years. All of a sudden, a barrage of rocks hit the roof of our hut, and some bounced off the walkway that went around it. The rocks had come from the Japanese hut. Right away, someone wanted to retaliate, but sounder judgment prevailed and that idea was dropped. Our new thought was: *Let's not press our luck just now!*

Hardly anyone slept that night, and at dawn we were ready to head for Nakhon Pathom. Shortly after dawn, the Japanese lieutenant came to our hut and in halting English tried to tell us about the atomic bomb. He motioned and gesticulated, trying to indicate an enormous explosion, but we just couldn't comprehend what he was trying to tell us. Finally, with tears in his eyes, he indicated that Japan had surrendered. He went on to tell us that he was to take us to Nakhon Pathom as soon as we were ready to go. He made it clear that he was to escort us to make sure that no other troops would harm us.

We got our gear on our shoulders and walked out to the road and started in the direction of Nakhon Pathom. We had walked more than halfway before the trucks that were to pick us up came down the road. We loaded into them and rode the rest of the way.

Excitement reigned supreme as we rode into the Nakhon Pathom camp. Just as we had been told, the flags of the allies in the Pacific—America, Britain, Holland, and Australia—were flying above the gate. The American flag was a handmade banner that had been put together by one of the men of the 131st, who had patiently collected cloth of the right colors and then had sewn them all together. The flag measured four feet by eight feet. I wasn't sure if the other flags were handmade, but I thought not. Inside the camp small flags were displayed on nearly all the huts.

Though in days past there had been times when the various nationalities had their differences, this was a day of brotherhood. It was like Christmas and the beginning of the school holidays all rolled into one. Almost hourly, new reports were being circulated through the camp that put the edge on our anticipation of being released and going home. Contact had been made with an OSS unit near Nakhon Pathom, and they were keeping the allied officers of the camp informed as to what was being done to get everyone out of Thailand and back to their homes. Of course, by the time some of the reports got to us, they were laced with many rumors; so it was hard to separate fact from someone's wildest dreams. Most of the first day was spent going about the camp and finding buddies I hadn't seen for some months.

On the second day, a report swept through the camp that all Americans were to be flown home. This information was dismissed, at first, as a wild rumor. Who ever heard of flying 600 to 800 guys home from halfway around the world? A couple of days later the story was confirmed—it was no rumor.

Just before noon on the second day, a bunch of us were sitting in a hut talking about all that we expected to do when we were free, when the sound of airplane motors drowned out our voices. "Boy, that one was low," commented one guy. "Yeah, it wasn't a bomber either," volunteered someone else. As the noise faded, we jumped to our feet and ran to the nearest door to look out and see what was happening. The sound of an approaching motor caught our attention and we looked to the south. There, flying at about 500 feet, was a two-motored C-47 cargo plane. Just as it cleared the south edge of the camp, several large bundles came tumbling out the door on the side of the plane, fell rapidly, hit the ground with a loud *crunch*, and slid for some 200 feet to a point directly between two huts.

As soon as they had stopped sliding, the packages were covered with scrambling humanity, snatching and grabbing at the ropes and laces that held the bundles together. In a moment the packages burst open and C-rations and K-rations spilled all over the ground. The hundreds of packages disappeared in seconds, it seemed, as hands grabbed in wild excitement. Of course, we had never heard of C-rations and K-rations, but it didn't take us long to learn that they meant food—and cigarettes.

The sound of motors in the air was heard again. Another plane was coming in for another drop. Three bundles hurtled toward the ground . . . *Plop! Plop! Plop!*. . .they hit and slid. Three or four Dutchmen ran out to stop them and were pushed aside like bowling pins as the 300-pound packages slid past them. Luckily, the eager men weren't hurt. As soon as the packages stopped, the scene of excited grabbing was repeated, and in just an instant there was nothing on the ground but the wrappings of the food bundles. These food drops continued on a daily basis and were still going on when I left the camp some three days later.

I had been in Nakhon Pathom for a couple of days and was

well aware of the plan to fly the Americans home, but I couldn't get my feelings to rise above the mere hope that the story was true. I was in a hut getting the addresses of Aussies that I wanted to stay in touch with when Eric Rogers, my Aussie buddy in the little camp at the bridge and ferry, came up and said that the story was really true. He also said that all Americans were to meet at the main camp office where they would be given the full details. I made my way to the main office, and as the group of 200 or so Americans stood there, we were told that we would be leaving the next morning. We would travel by truck to Rat Buri, where the Japanese had just completed an airstrip, and planes would come down from Calcutta to pick us up and fly us back to a hospital there. I don't recall that I slept that night. I don't think any of us did.

We were on the parade ground the next morning at eight o'clock, but there wasn't a truck to be seen. Nine o'clock, still no trucks. Finally, around ten o'clock, the trucks drove into camp. We scrambled aboard and in a few minutes we were on our way to Rat Buri. The trip took a couple of hours, so it was just after noon when we got to the airstrip. Some of the guys had worked on it and said that the Japanese had never used it—they hadn't had time.

A unit of OSS troops was there ahead of us; they had set up a radio station and were in contact with Calcutta. The commander of the unit was a cavalry captain and he was a rugged individual. As soon as the surrender had been announced, this unit had moved in on the airstrip from a small camp they had established some weeks before a couple of miles from the landing runway. They had taken all the Japanese there and put them in the small building that was meant to serve as an office.

We had arrived and were all gathering around the men of the OSS unit when we noticed that the ten or twelve Japanese that were being held in the building had come out the door to see what was going on. The captain saw them and yelled for them to get back inside because what we were doing was none of their business. They didn't move quickly enough to suit the captain, so he picked up a large chunk of wood lying nearby and threw it at them. They scrambled through the door and weren't hit, but a loud cheer went up from all of us. It was good to see the tables turned for a change.

After a short talk by the captain telling us what to expect, we lined up and were given a shelter half, a clean suit of khakis, soap, toothpaste, towels, and blankets. We would stay there until the next morning.

By the time everyone was bathed and had set up their pup tents, it was getting dark. I went to the radio tent and listened as the operator talked to Calcutta and got the instructions and plans that were to be carried out during the liberation operation. It was well after midnight when we finally went to bed. And, really, it wasn't as hard to go to sleep as we had thought it would be.

When we were routed out of bed the next morning, a big breakfast of C-rations was all warmed up for us. We ate and the captain told us that the planes, nine C-47s, would be in at nine o'clock. The time went by fairly fast and the next thing we knew a C-47 was circling the field. In just moments, eight more planes were in the pattern and began landing. They taxied up near the communications tent, lined up, and cut their motors. The officer in charge of the planes was in the first one, so he was ready, when all nine planes were on the ground, to brief the pilots. He had a short session with them, and then he turned to us and told us how we would load and what we could expect on the flight and so forth. And then we were loaded onto the planes.

We were surprised to see that the plane crew was so young. The pilot, we learned, was twenty-three and an air force colonel. The copilot was eighteen. The flight sergeant was thirty. The pilot had been told to fly at 8,000-feet altitude, but when he reached that altitude he decided it was too rough, so he went to 10,000 feet. We were happy to be flying at any altitude, but at 10,000 feet we were about to freeze. We had nothing on but shorts, and there were no blankets in the plane. We just sat there and froze but were happy.

We landed in Rangoon for lunch and then took off for Calcutta. We landed at Dumdum Airport late in the afternoon and were immediately loaded onto trucks and taken to an air force hospital. As we got off the trucks at the hospital, we were sprayed with DDT powder and then told to undress and get in the showers.

Many of us had brought out articles we considered to be

souvenirs. I had a Dutch water bottle that I had carried for the last couple of years. I left that in Rangoon. But I had come through with a couple of metal boxes, small ones that I carried tobacco in; a spoon I made from an American mess kit; and a wooden carving of an elephant that I wanted to give to my sister. The last time I had heard from any of my family, she was collecting such things. Also, I had an address book that I had made up during the last days at Nakhon Pathom. I lost my address book when I forgot to take it out of the pocket of the shorts I was wearing. When I thought about it, I rushed out to where we had piled our clothes as we went into the shower, but they were gone.

We spent ten hectic days in Calcutta. Then we were put aboard a plane and flown to Karachi, where we had a six- or eight-hour layover. Finally, about two o'clock in the afternoon, we were called and notified that our plane, a C-54, was ready for us to go aboard. We got on the plane, and some 20,000 miles and thirty-six hours later we landed at National Airport in Washington, DC. We were taken directly to the Bethesda Naval Hospital, where we were fed a sumptuous steak dinner—at one o'clock in the morning. Then we were assigned to a ward and put to bed. We stayed in Bethesda for about three weeks, and then we were sent to our respective homes on the first of many days of leave.

I walked up on my family's front porch in Corpus Christi, Texas, about one o'clock in the morning October 5, 1945—five years to the day after I had left in 1940.

Glossary

atap: thatch for native huts; made of nipa palm leaves
bagoose [banya bagus]: very good
baka, bakaro, bakarado [baka yaroo]: fool; idiot; blockhead
benjo: latrine; toilet
beoke [byooki]: sick; sickness
bungo: count off
carameta: pony cart
chunkle: broad-blade hoe
godown: warehouse
gula mullaca: palm sugar
ichi: one
jalang: run
kampong: hut; cluster of huts; small village
kari [keirei]: salute
kioski, kitoski [kisoku, kiritsu]: attention; get to one's feet
krises: daggers
kumi: squad; group
kumicho: squad or group leader
nandaka [doko ni doko]: where is it; in what place
ni: two
saki, sakika [sake]: alcoholic beverage; liquor
san: three
skoki, skokieda [kokooki]: plane; aircraft
tanko: muster
tatami: floor mat made of rice straw
ticals: Thai dollars
yasemae [yasumi]: rest day; holiday; at ease
yon: four
yo yo: bag and pole for moving dirt

[ ] = **Japanese spelling and definition**

Appendix A

Speech Delivered by Lt. Col. Y. Nagatomo to Allied Prisoners of War at Thanbyuzayat, Burma, on October 28, 1942

It is a great pleasure to me to see you at this place as I am appointed Chief of the war prisoners camp obedient to the Imperial Command issued by His Majesty the Emperor. The great East Asiatic war has broken out due to the rising of the East Asiatic Nations whose hearts were burnt with the desire to live and preserve their nations on account of the intrusion of the British and Americans for the past many years.

There is therefore no other reason for Japan to drive out the Anti-Asiatic powers of the arrogant and insolent British and Americans from East Asia in co-operation with our neighbors of China and other East Asiatic Nations and establish the Great East Asia Co-Prosperity Sphere for the benefit of all human beings and establish lasting great peace in the world. During the past few centuries, Nippon has made great sacrifices and extreme endeavors to become the leader of the East Asiatic Nations, who were mercilessly and pitifully treated by the outside forces of the British and Americans, and the Nippon Army, without disgracing anybody, has been doing her best until now for fostering Nippons real power.

You are only a few remaining skeletons after the invasion of East Asia for the past few centuries, and are pitiful victims. It is not your fault, but until your governments do not wake up from their dreams and discontinue their resistance, all of you will not be released. However, I shall not treat you badly for the sake of humanity as you have no fighting power left at all.

His Majesty the Emperor has been deeply anxious about all prisoners of war, and has ordered us to enable the opening of War Prisoner camps at almost all the places in the SW countries.

The Imperial Thoughts are unestimable and the Imperial Favors are infinite, and as such, you should weep with gratitude at the greatness of them. I shall correct or mend the misleading and improper Anti-Japanese ideas. I shall meet with you hereafter and at the beginning I shall require of you the four following points:

(1) I heard that you complain about the insufficiency of various items. Although there may be lack of materials it is difficult to meet your requirements. Just turn your eyes to the present conditions of the world. It is entirely different from the prewar times. In all lands and countries materials are considerably short and it is not easy to obtain even a small piece of cigarette and the present position is such that it is not possible even for needy women and children to get sufficient food. Needless to say, therefore at such inconvenient places even our respectable Imperial Army is also not able to get mosquito nets, foodstuffs, medicines and cigarettes. As conditions are such, how can you expect me to treat you better than the Imperial Army? I do not prosecute according to my own wishes and it is not due to the expense but due to the shortage of materials at such difficult places. In spite of our wishes to meet their requirements, I cannot do so with money. I shall supply you, however, if I can do so with my best efforts and I hope you will rely upon me and render your wishes before me. We will build the railroad if we have to build it over the white man's body. It gives me great pleasure to have a fast moving defeated nation in my power. You are merely rubble but I will not feel bad because it is your rulers. If you want anything you will have to come through me for same and there will be many of you who will not see your homes again. Work cheerfully at my command.

(2) I shall strictly manage all of your going out, coming back, meeting with friends, communications. Possessions of money shall be limited, living manners, deportment, salutation, and attitude shall be strictly according to the rules of the Nippon Army, because it is only possible to manage you all, who are merely rubble, by the order of military regulations. By this time I shall issue separate pamphlets of house rules of War prisoners and you are required to act strictly in accordance with these rules and you shall not infringe on them by any means.

(3) My biggest requirement from you is escape. The rules of escape shall naturally be severe. This rule may be quite useless and only binding to some of the war prisoners, but it is most important for all of you in the management of the camp. You should therefore be contented accordingly. If there is a man here who has at least 1% of a chance to escape, we shall make him face the extreme penalty. If there is one foolish man who is trying to escape, he shall see big jungles toward the East which are impossible for communication. Towards the West he shall see boundless ocean and above all, in the main points of the North, South, our Nippon Armies are guarding. You will easily understand the difficulty of complete escape. A few such cases of ill-omened matters which happened in Singapore (execution of over a thousand Chinese civilians) shall prove the above and you should not repeat such foolish things although it is a lost chance after great embarrassment.

(4) Hereafter, I shall require all of you to work as nobody is permitted to do nothing and eat at the present. In addition, the Imperial Japanese have great work to promote at the places newly occupied by them, and this is an essential and important matter. At the time of such shortness of materials your lives are preserved by the military, and all of you must award them with your labor. By the hand of the Nippon Army Railway Construction Corps to connect Thailand and Burma, the work has started to the great interest of the world. There are deep jungles where no man ever came to clear them by cutting the trees. There are also countless difficulties and suffering, but you shall have the honor to join in this great work which was never done before, and you shall also do your best effort. I shall investigate and check carefully about your coming back, attendance so that all of you except those who are unable to work shall be taken out for labor. At the same time I shall expect all of you to work earnestly and confidently henceforth you shall be guided by this motto.

Y. Nagatomo
Lieutenant Colonel, Nippon
Exp. Force
Chief No. 3 Branch
Thailand POW Administration

Appendix B

USS *Houston* (CA-30) Memorial Monument

Standing proudly in Sam Houston Park off Allen Parkway in Houston, Texas, is the USS *Houston* (CA-30) Memorial Monument which was dedicated on November 11, 1995, in a ceremony attended by some thirty-six survivors and more than two hundred next of kin.

After many years of dedicated and tireless effort on the part of the USS *Houston* Foundation Committee, a project of the Texas Commandery of The Naval Order of the United States, the monument will serve as an eternal memorial to the brave men who served aboard a gallant ship.

The sixteen-ton, five-sided monument of sunset-red Texas granite is inscribed with 1,068 names of the *Houston's* crew and is topped with the bell from the sunken ship. Brought up by Javanese divers in 1973 from a depth of 134 feet, the bell was first presented to the American ambassador in Java. The Navy then gave the bell to the city of Houston, and it was eventually displayed on the deck of the USS *Texas* at San Jacinto Battleground Park near Deer Park, Texas. When the *Texas* was later sent to dry-dock for a complete overhaul, the bell was stored away from public view. The Texas Commandery discovered that the bell was indeed in the ship's hold with no plans for future display, and arrangements were made for it to be placed in the Heritage Museum in Sam Houston Park. Several years later, through the continued efforts of the Commandery, the bell has now found a permanent resting place.

The construction of the monument was made possible by hundreds of individuals, veterans, businessmen and women, corporations, civic associations, and schoolchildren. The following are major donors: Battle Mountain Gold Company, Gallery Furniture, Houston Endowment, Inc., Houston Independent

School District, Mr. and Mrs. Paul N. Howell, Jim and Linda McIngvale, Shell Oil Company, Strake Foundation, Tenneco, Inc., USS *Stout* (DDG 55) Committee, and Bob Whorton. Special thanks also go to Continental Airlines, official airline for the USS *Houston* Foundation, Humphries Construction Corp., General Contractor, and Jackson & Ryan Architects.

Future plans are to hold an annual memorial service on the Saturday nearest March 1 each year. This tradition will be continued by members of The Next Generation: children, grandchildren, and other next of kin of the crew of the USS *Houston* (CA-30).

USS *HOUSTON* FOUNDATION COMMITTEE

Captain Carl V. Ragsdale, USN (RET), Chairman
Lieutenant Commander Clarke L. Coldren, USN (RET)
Captain Carter B. Conlin, USN (RET)
Captain Arthur R. Gralla, Jr., USN (RET)
Captain Cal Dean Hill, Jr., USN (RET)
Captain George W. Holyfield, USN (RET)
Commander William T. Kendall, USN (RET)
Mr. Raymond L. Nelson
Commander James B. Sterling, III, USN (RET)
Mayor Bob Lanier, Honorary Chairman

Crew of the USS Houston (CA 30)

L C ABATE • C E ABRAHAMSON • R E ABRAMS • C B ADAMS
R L ADAMS • B ADKINS • G L AGIN • F AH • A E AIRHART
A M ALBERS • H S ALBERS • B T ALBIN • E A ALBRECHT • H P ALDERMAN
C W ALFORD • E W ALLABAUGH • G L ALLEN • H B ALLEN • H R ALLEN
H A ALLEN JR • R R ALLEN • J G ALLEVA • M J ALLRED • J H ALMASIE
C B ANDERSON • J W ANDERSON JR • R H ANDERSON
D Z ANDREWS JR • R W ANGLIN • R H ANGLIN • G B ANSPAUGH
A L ANTHONY • C D ARGO JR • F ARMOUR • R ARNESON
F V ARNOLD • M L ASHMEAD • C E ASHTON • J C ASHTON
C T ATTERBERRY • R AUST JR • R E AUSTON • L E AUTIO • J G AUTREY
P S AWTREY • W C AXELSON • R C AYERS • C A BACK JR • A J BACKER
D G BAERMAN • I W BAILEY • J H BAILEY • L W BAILEY • M L BAIN
T W BAIZE • G D BAKER • G W BAKER • W S BAKER • J L BALLEW
J M BALLINGER • E M BARRETT • H T BARBATTI • S D BARNES • R I BARNETT
D M BARNEY • G M BARR • N S BARRETT • R BARRETT • E F BARRINGER
F W BARRON • J E BARTZ • R A BASSETT • W C BATCHLOR • L F BATTLES
N W BAUGH • M M BEARDSLEY • J R BEATTY • P E BEATTY • O C BECK
R A BECKETT • W J BEDFORD • W L BLESON • J R BELL • G F BENDER
L R BENJAMINE • C W BENNER • S J BERGAM • J T BERGEN
A C BERHASEK JR • P J BETTINGER • V B BEVEL JR • L E BIECHLIN
N C BIECHLIN • J B BIENERT • D B BIGGER • W E BINDER JR • J L BINGHAM
H L BINGLEY • L C BIRD • V A BISHOP • A R BLACK • I A BLACK
J G BLACK JR • S E BLACKFORD • K S BLAIR • P R BLAKE • F W BLOCH
D C BOCK • C L BOLT • J A BONKOSKI • E L BOONE • R W BOOROM
C W BOOTH • M A BOOTHE • T BORGHETTI JR • W R BOTHAM
D L BOUCHER • F J BOURGEOIS • W E BOWLBY • M R BOWLER
B G BOWMAN • D E BOYNTON • W S BOZ • J W BRAATHEN • L E BRADLEY
D C BRAIN • L F BRANDT • L R BRANHAM • W L BRASFIELD • R J BRILL
C M BRISLIN JR • C A BROCKMAN • HR BROOKS • H E BROOKS • D C BROOM
F W BROTHERS • A R BROWN JR • D C BROWN • H F BROWN • H L BRUCE
J L BURST • J A BUBNIS • L A BUCKNER • C N BUHLMAN • W A BUICE
S F BUJAK • E G BUKOWSKI • J BULLA JR • J J BUNCH • V L BUNNELL
A H BUNS • B C BUNYARD • C N BURGARD • J BURGE • J O BURGE
F V BURNS • C D BURROUGHS • D F BURRELL • R B BURRELL • F E BURTON
E A BUSH • A G BUSHELL • E W BUSHNELL • C J BUTTON • J R BYRD
D J BYRNE • R CALLAWAY • L A CALLAHAN • M C CALLAHAN
M J CALLAHAN • A M CALVERT • C B CAMPBELL • J F CAMPBELL • R L CAMPBELL
W E CAMPBELL • J A CANTRELL • T S CANTRILL • J CAPLICKY • C E CARLSON
E T CARLYLE • G R CARNEY • C E CARROLL • R L CARSILLO • F L CARTER
G G CARTER • A CASE • E R CASERIO • L F CASEY • J L CASH
W R CASSADAY • M CASTRO • L F CATON • S J CEBLAK • J E CERRUTI
J C CHAMBLISS • G CHAN • R C CHANDLER • T K CHANDLER • S A CHANG
G T CHAPMAN • H R CHARLES • W CHAY • C R CHEADLE • C S CHENG
S S CHENG • C M CHERRY JR • T J CHERRY • A CHIE • K C CHIE
L CHIEN • S CHIH • M K CHILDERS • Y C CHING • J K CHISHOLM

Crew of the USS Houston (CA 30)

C L CHORMAN • S F CHOW • L A CHRISTENSEN • D R CLARK
P R CLARK • W T CLARK • L O CLARKSTON • D CLINGINGSMITH
S H CLYMER • J R COBLE • E J CODERRE • P L COLBERT • U H COLBERT
C M COLLINGS • R E COLLINS • L D COLLITON • J G COMER
J H CONNELL • M E CONNER • W A CONNER • J F COOK • D R COOPER
L F COOPER • J L COPELAND • H C CORSBERG • J R CRAVENS
H R CRAY JR • J CREED • H E CREPPS JR • M E CRIPPEN • E C CRISPI
H CUMMING JR • M F CURNUTTE • C CZYZENSKY • M W DAGGET
R M DALEY • C E DALTON • J F DALTON • T D DANIELS • W W DANIELS
W E DARLING • J R DARTER • T A DAVIDSON • C B DAVIS • G E DAVIS JR
H E DAVIS • J S DAVIS • S C DAVIS • C N DAY • R DAY • M A DEBORD
E E DEFRANTES • A R DEMOEN • D D DEMOSS • W M DESHIELDS
F A DETHLOFF • R L DETHLOFF • G E DETRE • W C DEWALD • R E DEXTER
L L DICKERSON JR • J C DICKIE • N W DIETRICH • E J DIETZ • J E DILLON
C P DINAN • T P DITTOE • M DOBKINS • L C DODDS
E S DOMBROWSKI • G W DONAHOU • T R DORRELL • R DOTSON
C DOTY • G L DOUGLAS • T A DOWELL • W L DOWLING • D T DRAGO
M L DRAKE • T DUCEY • A R DU HAIME • R H DUMAS • H H DUPLER
O J DURLER • A J DUTTON • B V DYKES • S F DYMANOWSKI • J D EARLY
E M EBAUGH • F V EBAUGH • M V EDDY • J W EDGE • J F EDWARDS
D W EGELSTON • G J EGRI • H G EIDEN • O D EKBERG • R W ELAM
C F ELLIOTT • L L ELLIOTT • F D ELLIS • L G ELMS • W H EMMERTH
H A ENGLISH • W A EPSTIEN • R L ERMIS • J M EUGATES • M J EUSTACE
J C EWING • G FANGHOR • B R FANNON • F M FARNSWORTH
J H FAULK • E C FAUST • H L FAY • J J FEELY • L J FEIGLE • J P FELDSCHER
O FELICE • I A FELIX • J M FELIZ • J A FERGUSON • S FEUCHACK
J G FINCHER • J R FITZGERALD • G P FLANIGAN • R C FLORENCE
H L FLOWERS • D C FLYNN • W J FONTENOT • L FOOK • R W FORNKAHL
J E FORRESTER • M L FORSMAN • C P FOWLER • H M FRANTZ • R J FREEMAN
R L FRITZSCHING • R W FROELICH • W L FROST • R B FULTON II • D E FUSSEL
J H FUSSEL • G GAGNON JR • W J GALBRAITH • F E GALLAGHER JR
L H GALOWSKI • E R GALUSHA • G L GALYEAN • C W GANDY • P T GANS
J J GARRETT • W E GARRETT • E D GARWOOD • J C GARY JR • J W GEE
S C GENTRY JR • K B GEORGE • M E GEORGE • P M GEORGE • A V GERKE JR
L A GIBBON • J E GIBSON • J P GILLELAND • F A GILLET • L O GILLIAM
C E GILLMORE • A J GIRET • R M GLOVER • D F GODFREY • W F GOODBERLET
R GOODSON • J P GORE • R T GORNEY • J P GRAHAM • R G GRAHAM
J B GRAHAM • C H GRANGER • L B GRANT • S J GRASHAM • J D GRAY
E F GREEN • W L GRICE • E F GRIFFIN • R H GINGRAS • H S GRODZKY
C E GUERNSEY • A D GUGLIETTI • C F GUNNERSON • J A GUY • F G GUYER
P GYUGO JR • J W HAINLINE • E L HALL • M C HALL • R F HALL • J M HAMILL
H S HAMLIN JR • D M HANKINSON • R L HANLEY • R R HANSEN • C H HANSON
R J HANSON • J H HARDER • D HARGRAVE • R D HARNDEN JR • W R HAROLD
D J S HARPER • D H HARRELL • J A HARRELL • P HARRINGTON • L H HARRIS
W D HASKEL • E A HATLEN • D W HAWKINS • J B HAWKINS • G W HAYES

Crew of the USS Houston (CA 30)

G E HAZEN • T V HEAVEY • M R HEBERT • G R HEDRICK JR
R H HENDRICKS • D F HENLY • R J HERMAN • B HIDDENGA
H W HIETT • D D HIGHFILL • C G HILL • D W HILL • E E HINMAN
A A HIRSCH • H HIRSCH • L HIRSCHBERG • R G HITTLE • C H HO
M H HOBBS • E D HODGE • J E HOGAN • J J HOGUE
L N HOLLINGSWORTH • J A HOLLOWELL JR • H C HOLM • J H HOLMES JR
F O HOLSINGER • J E HOOD • E F HOOFER • L R HOOPER
E N HOSTICK • D A HOUSTON • M A HOUT • F M HOWARD • R HOWARD
W R HUBBARD • E A HUEBLER JR • J W HUFFMAN • S E HULT • R K HUMBLE
E C HUMPHREY • L C HUNTER • M C HURD • G N HUSEK • L T HURRELL
B M HUTCHINSON • W H HYSER • W INGRAM JR • E C ISAACS • J IVEY
J J IWANICKI • S J IWANICKI • E JACKSON • P JACOBS JR • E R JAMES
H W JAMES JR • N B JELLISON • F C JENKINS • M W JOHNK • A L JOHNSON
D R JOHNSON • E I JOHNSON • E E JOHNSON • H M JOHNSON
J C JOHNSON • N E JOHNSON • R R JOHNSON • W L JOHNSON
W JOHNSON • W A JOHNSON • M L JONES • W S JONES • J B JONTZ
R G JORDAN • H M JUSTICE • J KADLEC • B R KAISER • T J KAMLER
C J KANE • A L KARBONSKI • R KALINOWSKI • C A KAUTTER • W KEAST
O J KEEN JR • S C KEI • K C KEIFER • F W KEITH • A M KELLEY • F T KELLEY
H T KELLEY • A W KENRICK • A E KENNEDY • J KENNY • R E KETMAN JR
J KEYNO • K C KIEFER • M T KIELTY • S KIERTIANIS • F H KING
J W KING • V N KING • J N KIRINCICH • H G KIRKPATRICK • W A KIRKPATRICK
R L R KLYMAZEWSKI • D W KNOLL • J T KNOWLETON • B F KOCHER
V L KOELLING • V G KOENIG • F E KOEPKEY • W P KOHL • F KOHN
J R KOLLER • K L KOLLMYER • L F KONDZELA • A KOO • Y F KOO
L W KOOPER • A KOPP • J KORMOS • G P KOSKI • T KRASMIZEH
R G KRASS • R A KRAUS • A KREKAN • C L KULIBERT • I A KULIBERT
Y KUN • C J KUNKE • C D KVACH • G H KYLE • J F LACHMAN
J A LAFFERTY • J R LAIRD • A S LAM • J D LAMADE • R V LAMB • F W LAMM
A W LANIGAN • C J LANN • W C LANTZ • C W LATTIN • G W LAWSON
G F LAYNE JR • A V LEDBETTER • E H LEE • J F LEE • R LEE • W G LEE
E E LEHNHOFF • N LEO • W LEVCHENKO • H A LEVITT • J LEWDANSKY
D M LEWIS • J A LEWIS • S S LIEBLA • Z F LIEN • A J LINDSLEY • J A LINDSTROM
B E LINDSTAEDTER • F J LOCJNER • J A LOFLAND • W E LOGAN • C W W LOHRIG
L G LOUIS • J LUNA • J M T LUSK • E T LUTES • C L LYNCH • H V LYONS
J P MABRY • R J MACDONALD • F L MACUMBER • Q C MADSON • A L MAHER
M H MAHLANDT • L H MAINY • P MAKRIS • F F MALLORY • A K MALONE
G F MAMER • T MANION JR • A MANISTA • M M MARINOS • L W MARSH
S J MARSH • W L MARSH JR • A M MARTIN • J E MARTIN • P MARTIN
R I MARTIN • V MARTIN • A MARTINEZ • B MARTON • P W MARTWICK
T H MARVEL • A O MASSEY • F C MATTHEWS • J M MATHIEU • E V MAY
M R MAY • C A MAYO III • G C MCCANDLESS • O T MCCARTY • J E MCCLASKEY
J MCCONE • P M MCDONALD • E L MCFADDEN • T J MCFARLAND
T J MCFARLANE • E A MCFEE • A E MCGARVEY • L V MCGEHEE • R P MCGRANN
C J MCKENZIE • H H MCMANUS • O C MCMANUS • S T MCMASTER

Crew of the USS Houston (CA 30)

M D MCMULLIN • J G MCNEALY • E J MEREDITH • L R MESNER
A W METZGER • W C MIETH • W R MILES • J L MILGEL • C W MILLER
H E MILLER • J V MILLER • F L MILLER • W D MILLER • W D MILLER
F J MILLS • S MILLS • O C MINTON • R J MOGA • E J MONTGOMERY
L MOODY JR • C I MOON • H L MOORE • J T MORRIS • R N MORRIS
C V MOUNT • W D MULLINS • A R MURFF • J W MUSTO • S F MYERS
A R NEBEL • A H NEITCH • J D NELSON • J B NELSON • J W NELSON
K L NELSON • A F NETHKEN • J G NETTER • F R NEWEL • W A NEWTON
W D NEWTON • H NICKEL • R NICKELSON • A NICOLAO
G NIEDERHOUS • D K NIES • D L NISWONGER • J A NORTHCUTT
R NORVEL • S E NOVICKI • E B NOWAK • R B NUNNELLEY
J F O'BRIEN • R L O'BRIEN • E P O'HAYRE • E L O'LEARY • W M OLIVER JR
R E OMOTH • J S O'NEAL • R Y ORCUTT • E ORTH • J G OVERTURF
F I OWENS • G N OWENS • W L OWENS • E P OXFORD • J O PACQUIN
B E PAGE JR • E PANGANIBAN • P E PAPISH • T E PARHAM
B H PARISH • C E PARKER • C E PARSONS • J E PATAYE • K B PATTEN
J C PATTY • P W PAUTSCH • T B PAYNE • T F PECENA • J PERKINS
E PERRY • C A PETERS • I E PETERS • L O PETERSON • R E PETERSON
D S PHILLIPS • A D PIERCE • W E PINKERMAN • F L PISTOLE
S PITCHON • C B PITTMAN • L PLUDE • R P POIRIER • V F POLIDORO
F G POLK • W E POOL • J J PORTER • L PRATICO • J H PRENTICE
H H PRESCHER • F D PRICE • C W PRINCE • W D PROUTY • C L PRYOR JR
R H PULLEN • M C PURCELL • G E PYE • F B QUICK • R A QUIGLEY
J J RACINE • D S RAFALOVICH • J E RAINS • F H RAMSEY • J W RANGER
J E RAYMAN • H R READ • J C REAS • P A REBURN • C O REED • N REED
R W REED • S D REESE • L W REHFELD • J J REIDER • J D REILLY
R R REISINGER • G S RENTZ • E L REVES • J E REYNOLDS • F RHODES
W A RHODES • G L ROACH • H D ROACH • W ROBE • N L ROBERSON
D W ROBERTS • V S ROBERTS • R N ROBERTSON • J W ROBINSON JR
M E ROBINSON • E D ROCHFORD • G T ROCQUE • L RODGERS
L RODY • F ROGERS • L W ROGERS • M J ROHRBRAUGH
J W ROLAND • A ROLF • A H ROOKS • G M ROSE • J J ROSE
R R ROSS • W ROSS JR • L T ROZELL • J T ROTH • R H ROWAN JR
J R RUDDY • J RUSCOE • R C RUSHING • M B RUSSELL • H J SADOWSKI
J H SALLIS • T SANDERCOOK • R SANDERS • C A SASS • R E SAUNDERS
R C SAWER • D E SCHANTZ • J W SCHERTZ • C H SCHILPROORT
C M SCHLOSSER • M W SCHMITT • W K SCHNECK • W B SCHNITIZIUS
T SCHRAM • J H SCHRODER JR • J H SCHUELKE • L O SCHUFFENHAUER
R P SCHULTZ • F B SCHULTZE • T SCHWAMLE • O C SCHWARZ
J F SCHWERS • D T SCOTT JR • L F SEATON • A G SEIDEL • C SELLERS IV
L E SELLERS • H D SHAW • K L SHAW • J K SHEARER • L A SHEFFIELD
R L SHELTON • S W SHEMANSKI • C A SHETTLESWORTH • G A SHILLINGS
F F SHIPMAN • C H SHIPPY • R L SHIREMAN • C A SHORT • C F SHOUSE
C W SHUMAKER • J F SHUSTER • J H SILER • T L SITTON • M SIZEMORE
B D SKIDMORE • A J SKINNER • J J SKUDLAS • J E SLOCUM • A J SMITH

Crew of the USS Houston (CA 30)

C D SMITH II • C F SMITH • E F SMITH • G G SMITH • H P SMITH
H P SMITH • J D SMITH • J L SMITH • J A SMITH • J R SMITH
L R SMITH • S D SMITH • S L SMITH • T B SMITH • W Q SMITH
W G SMITH • W S SMITH • E J SNYDER • S E SNYDER • W J SODEN JR
R A SOLBERGER • E N SORENSON • I G SOULE • A SOY
R L SPARKS • C L SPENCER • M D SPENCER • A J SPILLMAN
G W SPRAGLE • R M SPHAGUE • J G SPRAYBERRY • K SPRINKLE
W F STAFFORD • J C STAHL • J STANCZAK • W STANDISH
J N STARK • M C STARR • E W STEELE • J B STEFANEK • N E STEVENS
W W STEVENS JR • H V STEVENSON • G B STEWART • W J STEWART
J B STIVERS • G D STODDARD • F E STOKER • H H STONE • L T STORIE
D G STOWER • R A STREET • H S STRICKLAND • O J STURGILL • M SU
S W SUOMI • D G SWANSON • L W SWARTZ • L D SWEARINGEN
A S SZARKE • V J SZYMALA • C F TAI • A N TANNBERG
S TARASZKIEWICZ • E L TARRENCE • C L TAYLOR • E J TEMPLEMAN
A H TERRY • H TESAR • W E TETTERTON • W L THAXTON • H P THEW
C L THOMAS • E W THOMPSON • D J TIEFEL • W V TISDALE • H J TREANON
E M TRICE • D F TRIM • T F TRUSKOSKI • C L TSAO • D TSAO
P TSIANG • N D TSONG • R L TUBBS • W E TUCKER • V Y TUNG
R C TURMAN • J L TUTAS • L TYE • A W TYRE • S L UDITSKY • J J UKENA
R D USHER • S H USTAASZENSKI • H F VALLIERE • K A VANCIL
A E VANDENBERG • R J VANDER AUWER • R M VAN SLYKE
F E VAN TILBERG • H A VAUGHN • J H VAUGHN JR • R A VERLEY
J J VERZWYVELT • D D VILLERS • H H VILLWOCK • H M VINJE
H H VIRCHOW • L W VOGT • Y WAI • W W WAITE • H WALCHUK
A H WALDSCHMIDT JR • J G WALLACE • R T WALLEN • N C WALLING
H L WALTS • C A WAMPLER • F C WARD • W G WARD • L R WARGOWSKY
A E WARKEN • J C WARNER • C W WASHBURN JR • C H WATKINS
J E WATT • B E WEAVER • C T WEAVER • D C WEAVER • E M WEBER
R S WEEKS • F B WEILER • A G WEIMER • W J WEISSINGER JR
E A WESTFELT • A F WELLBOURN • M E WELLER • R A WENHOLTZ
P W WERNER JR • D H WESTERFIELD • R WEYGANT • J W WEYL
J H WHALEY • R S WHALEY • L H WHEELER • C E WHITE
G D WHITE • J H WHITE • W C WHITE • W A WHITEHEAD • G H WHITNEY
H C WIDMEYER • R M WIENERT • R L WILDER • R H WILEMON
G M WILEY JR • M W WILKER • E T WILKINSON • W O WILLENBERG
R P WILLERTON • L V WILLEY • A T WILLIAMS • A WILLIAMS
C H WILLIAMS • D M WILLIAMS • E D WILLIAMS • J M WILLIAMS • J A WILLIAMS
R O WILLIAMS • D W WILLIS • J L WILSON • J R WILSON • O W WILSON
P E WILSON • S S WILSON • W L WILSON • W G WINSLOW • J WINTERS
V WINTERS • G E WISE • R H WISE JR • J R WISECUP • L H WITTKOP
A W WOLF • F N WOLF • J W WOLF • G R WOLFE • M A WOLFE JR • A J WOLOS
F Z WONG • S W WOOD • J F WOODRUFF • S D WOODY • M E WOOTEN
M A WYNN • C YANNUCCI • R L YARBRO • D N YATES • K A YOUNG
W E ZABLER • J J ZAZZARA • W L ZELLER • L J ZIMBA • L ZIMMERMAN

INDEX